16 Septr

To My esteemed friend
Robert McFriese
with best wishes

J. J. "Jocko" Clark

Sea Power
and Its Meaning

THE WATTS SEA POWER LIBRARY

Sea Power and Its Meaning

by Admiral J. J. Clark, USN
and Captain Dwight H. Barnes, USNR

Revised Edition

Franklin Watts, Inc.
575 Lexington Avenue
New York, N.Y. 10022

As long as command of the seas is maintained by the Democracies, there is no danger of the world becoming totalitarian. . . .

—Admiral Harry E. Yarnell

FIRST PRINTING
REVISED EDITION
Copyright © 1966, 1968 by Franklin Watts, Inc.
Library of Congress Catalog Card Number: 66-18674
Manufactured in the United States of America

Contents

Contents

Sea Power
and Its Meaning

Foreword

By
ADMIRAL ARTHUR W. RADFORD
Former Chairman
Joint Chiefs of Staff

The Sea Power Library was initiated by publisher Franklin Watts with the cooperation of the Navy Department for the purpose of stimulating interest in the seas that surround us and of making us aware of the economic, political, social, and military dependence of the United States upon the oceans of the world.

The United States is the world's richest "have-not" nation. In spite of its tremendous industrial wealth, which has advanced it to the undisputed position of leadership in the free world, the United States lacks many raw materials necessary for our well-being, for our very survival. These must be brought from foreign lands across the oceans in the holds of ships. This economic dependence upon imported goods has not been realized adequately by the people of this nation.

Militarily, for reasons quite understandable, the purpose and operation of land forces and land-based air forces are more readily comprehended by the public than is the subject of sea power. We live on the land and we are creatures of it. Except for those people living near the shores, the general public has few opportunities ever to see the fleets of warships and merchant vessels which perform such essential roles in America's diplomacy, defense, and economy. Thus, we associate our thoughts with things we see and experience. This failure to look beyond our immediate surroundings is compounded by the fact that too few people have written about the sea, its threats, its promises, and its mysteries.

1

At the moment, we are living through one of civilization's most dangerous yet promising periods. The sea offers the equivalent of a new frontier of undeveloped resources. It also offers flexibility and numerous options which are not otherwise available to our policy makers in the formation of national and allied strategy. The one central fact that none dare overlook is the expanding interest of the Soviet Union in maritime matters, both commercial and naval. The Red giant of Eurasia is rapidly becoming the world's strongest commercial maritime power, sailing the biggest and most modern merchant fleet. Soviet military leaders continue to develop and build the most advanced instruments of warfare, with great emphasis on submarines, missiles, aircraft, nuclear propulsion, and nuclear weapons.

Prudence dictates that the United States and her allies deal with the actual military capabilities and possible courses of action rather than the assumed intentions of any potential adversary. We must, therefore, maintain an adequate navy to keep the sea-lanes open.

This book represents a concise, comprehensive, readable, and global treatment of sea power. It deals not only with the present but also includes the broad sweep of naval progress—from oars to nuclear propulsion—which will serve to inspire the students of history to give greater attention to the sea. To all citizens of America it stresses the importance of not only control of the sea but the future use of the world's oceans as highways of commerce. In addition, it sets forth the prospects of obtaining food and other commodities from the seas and beneath the seas.

Both the authors of this volume are especially qualified to write of sea power and its meaning. Admiral J. J. "Jocko" Clark, USN (Ret.) is one of the most able and colorful combat leaders of our Navy. Captain Dwight Barnes is one of our distinguished Reserve officers who represents a commendable blend of a highly successful civilian and military careerist. I am certain that readers will find this book both stimulating and rewarding.

⚓

CHAPTER ONE

A Four-Ocean Challenge

The last half of the twentieth century has truly become the Age of Space. As man moves forward on this new frontier, the romance of outer space causes many people with their heads among the stars to forget that their feet are planted firmly on the ground. Important as outer space may be, we must all live here on the earth together, along with three billion of our neighbors. By the end of this century, it is likely that there will be twice that many people in the world, for such is the explosive nature of our population growth. And since there is serious doubt that any portion of this mass of humanity ever will move to another planet, we must find adequate room here on earth for these people, each of whom will require a place to live, work, and play. The complexity of the problem is magnified to the nth degree by the fact that we can use for this purpose only 25 per cent of the earth's surface. Why? Because the other three fourths of the world is covered with water—140 million square miles of it. Actually, man lives only on islands—some big enough to be called continents—surrounded by vast expanses of water.

To appreciate this fact, one must discard the traditional flat maps —the Mercator projections—which have been used to teach geography down through the years. These distort the size of landmasses at higher latitudes and fail to reflect the true globular and oceanic nature of the world. Columbus to the contrary, Mercator projections have made us forget that the world is round.

Let us turn instead to a globe. Spin the globe while resting a finger lightly upon it. The odds are three to one that when the globe stops spinning, the color under your finger will be blue—blue water.

3

The spinning globe discloses some of the geographic facts of life which determine the pattern of economic, political, and military power in the world today. The capitals of Europe are closer to Washington, D.C., than some capitals in our own Western Hemisphere. Leningrad is about the same distance from New York as is Rome. Paris is as close to Moscow as New Orleans is to Los Angeles. The distance which separates South America from Africa is not much greater than that from San Francisco to the Mississippi River. On standard Mercator maps, Russia and China appear half a world removed from the United States. On a globe, only the short distance over the North Pole separates the two great military powers of East and West.

The spinning globe also discloses the most predominant geographic fact of our missile age. The broad expanses of the Atlantic and Pacific oceans, which once isolated the United States from military attack, can be spanned by nuclear armed ballistic missiles in a scant few minutes. But the fact remains that in war or peace, these oceans are wide barriers to the movement of any significant amount of manpower, strategic supplies, raw materials, or manufactured goods required for our international and domestic commerce. These vital necessities must still cross the seas in 15-knot ships.

Although the United States faces both the Atlantic and Pacific oceans, the former has been of primary interest to this nation since the days of our independence. A momentary failure of the British to maintain superior forces in the western Atlantic led to the defeat of Cornwallis and successfully ended our War of Independence. The War of 1812 was fought over the issue of freedom of the seas in the Atlantic and the Caribbean. In our own century, Germany almost won two European land wars by superb use of undersea craft with which she almost shut off the transatlantic lifeline of American supplies to our allies.

Encompassing 32 million square miles, the Atlantic is the second largest ocean in the world, but its size is not its most important feature. More vital is the community of nations that border the Atlantic. In the north, they are the industrial centers of our Western civilization and in the south they are the resource-rich emerging

4

nations of Africa and Latin America. The Atlantic is the main high-way of commerce binding together old and new nations which conduct more than two thirds of the world's merchant shipping. This makes the North Atlantic the most heavily traveled stretch of water in the world. More than two thousand merchant vessels are sailing North Atlantic trade routes every day of the year.

When viewed from the Pacific Ocean hemisphere, the earth appears to be virtually all water, so broad is the expanse of this mighty ocean. Landmasses are visible only on the fringes in this view of the world.

5

In size, however, the Atlantic is small when compared to the Pacific Ocean, which body of water is unequaled in vastness by any other land or sea mass. Sixty-seven million square miles of Pacific Ocean cover more than a third of the surface of the world. The Pacific equals the combined areas of the Atlantic, Indian, and Arctic oceans, and it also exceeds in area the total of all the landmasses of the world. Asia and North America are separated by only 67 miles at the northern extremes; then these continents veer sharply away from each other so that at the Equator the Pacific is more than 10,500 miles wide. The north–south span of the Pacific is more than 7,500 miles. By its very size, the Pacific influences the strategic thinking and planning of every nation bordering upon it. In World War II, the great distances created major logistic problems and dictated the United States' island-hopping strategy of leapfrogging to victory.

A third ocean bordering the North American continent has achieved strategic importance because of the development of nuclear power. Entry of nuclear submarines into the Arctic Ocean opened this 5.5-million-square-mile battleground on top of the world. The impact of this breakthrough can best be appreciated by again turning to the globe. With the Arctic Ocean becoming a naval operating area, the whole of the Soviet Union and the Eurasian continent becomes exposed to the influence of sea power sailing the international waters to the north where the Soviet Union has its longest coastline.

The Arctic Ocean and the Northwest Passage first became an elusive object for explorers in 1497, when Henry VII of England commissioned John Cabot to seek the northern route around the Island of the Americas. Cabot failed, however, and so did his son Sebastian, in 1509. Thereafter, explorers on the same mission were unsuccessful for nearly four centuries until the Norwegian Roald Amundsen sailed his tiny sloop *Gjøa* northward from the Atlantic to the Pacific, in a transit which took thirty-nine months of fighting ice and sea. The first passage of the Arctic Ocean was completed in August, 1906. Fifty-two years later, on August 3, 1958, the USS *Nautilus*, commanded by Captain W. R. Anderson, sailed under the North Pole on history's first undersea transit from the Pacific to the Atlantic.

6

The fact that this route cuts four thousand miles from the sea-lane distance between London and Tokyo achieves special significance in view of advanced studies now in process on the development of submarine cargo carriers. Even today commercial shipping operations are not unknown in the Arctic. The Soviet Union has been using the northern sea route from Europe to Asia since 1928. Moreover, nuclear-powered icebreakers may extend the brief season in which this route is open to travel.

The underside of the Eurasian continent has always been susceptible to pressures from the seas. For centuries, the Indian Ocean has been an arena for competing powers vying for the riches of South Asian shores. Twenty-eight million square miles of ocean stretch from Malaysia to Africa, an area which is home to a third of the world's peoples.

At the outset of any discussion of sea power, the physical composition of our oceanic world must be fully appreciated. Basic to this consideration is the fact that ocean areas are so extensive that all landmasses on earth are vulnerable to attack or pressure from the sea. So broad is the impact of sea power.

To fully comprehend this, we must explore the landmasses upon which we live. Most are insular in nature. The nations of England and Japan have always been recognized as islands. Early in history their people were forced by lack of natural resources and geographic location to take full advantage of the seas. They developed naval and merchant fleets capable of dominating not only their home waters, but also large ocean areas. This gave England, which is smaller than the state of Florida, and Japan, which is about the size of the state of Montana, tremendous influence over the later development of world history. Their influence was felt especially on the continental landmasses opposite them.

Yet the people of England and Japan comprise only a small fraction of those living on insular landmasses today. The continents of North and South America must be considered as two separate "islands" tied together only by the thin strand called the Isthmus of Panama. Africa is nearly surrounded by the Atlantic and Pacific oceans, and the Red and Mediterranean seas. But the true mark of

7

their insular nature is the dependence of these continents upon the seas for their very existence.

Each of the continental islands owes its initial development to economic and military sea power exercised by smaller insular or peninsular nations seeking to exploit newly discovered natural resources. For example, the search for raw materials, colonies, and naval bases abroad led England to North American shores. Spanish sea power sailed westward to Central and South America for gold, silver, and other riches needed to sustain a rising empire. Later, European maritime nations turned southward to exploit the resources of Africa.

Today, South America and Africa continue to be the primary suppliers of the natural resources consumed by the industrial regions of the free world. Much of our cobalt comes from Africa. The Union of South Africa ranks second only to the Soviet Union in the production of gold. The world's largest deposits of manganese and important newly discovered iron fields are located on the African continent. Although the potential for further development of resources remains virtually unlimited, Africa has little or no transportation facilities in its interior. Travel is limited largely to available inland and coastal waterways. As a result, two thirds of the capitals of all the nations and dependencies of Africa are located within 100 miles of the 100,000-mile stretch of coastline.

Vast in territory and diverse in climate, South America abounds with productive lands which can raise almost any farm product. Agriculture accounts for more than 25 per cent of the gross national product and absorbs more than half the labor force. Coffee, of course, is the South American crop closest to the hearts of North Americans. United States coffee imports exceed one billion dollars annually. Drugs and rubber are two critical forest products of South America. In addition to the gold, silver, and precious stones which first attracted the Spanish *conquistadores*, many other minerals vital to present-day economies are attaining increasing importance. Brazil has a quarter of the world's iron. Chile has the largest copper deposits anywhere. Bolivia mines 15 per cent of the world's tin. Venezuela is one of the world's largest exporters of oil. And manganese, vanadium, chrome, and nitrates are all found in great quantity in South America.

However, South America's development is also plagued by inadequate transportation. Dominated by the towering 4,000-mile-long Andes Range, South America is divided geographically, commercially, and politically. Thus, Latin Americans must also turn seaward

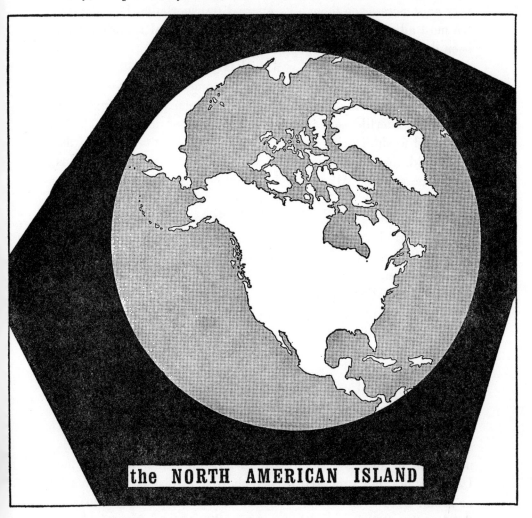

the NORTH AMERICAN ISLAND

Geographically, the North American continent can easily be visualized as an "island." Politically and economically we must also look outward across the seas for continued existence in an oceanic world.

for their communications, trade, and transport—even between points on their own continent.

From all this, one must conclude that the political and economic destinies of these great continents and their nearly 420 million people are indeed insular in nature and are tied to the oceans.

As for North America, it too is dependent upon the seas for its very existence—even though its internal transportation facilities are the most advanced in the world and its rich natural resources have been developed to a high degree.

Initially, this continent was settled largely because its resources were needed in Europe. The fledgling colonies which later became part of the United States were blessed geographically with favorable climate and fertile soil. They soon outdistanced the parent lands of the old world. During this transition from colony to leader of the free world, there was a period of relative self-sufficiency. This, plus the vastness of the Atlantic and Pacific oceans, lulled some North Americans into the political complacency of isolationism. But this was only a passing phase, for the United States always has truly been a maritime trading nation, taking full advantage of its long coastlines and excellent harbors. Its greatest growth has been achieved during periods of strong international maritime competition and active political internationalism.

While the United States has become the dominant nation in an industrialized and automated world, it has at the same time become more dependent upon sea transport and trade than ever before in its history. Climate, soil, and agricultural technology have been combined to make the United States produce huge agricultural surpluses of wheat, cotton, and other farm commodities which must be exported to maintain economic stability. At the same time, American science and industry have developed great demands for raw materials not found in adequate supply within the continental limits of the United States, nor produced by neighbors immediately to the north or south. Despite its strong economic and geographic position and the fact that it is bounded by oceans and nonaggressive neighbors, the United States still depends upon many distant countries for the raw materials needed for its defense and consumer industries. Naturally, the United States is generally committed to the physical defense of these same nations. The only physical link with this oceanic alliance is the sea. Therefore, the United States, too, must be considered insular in nature.

Thus it is apparent that geography forces dependence of these three insular continents upon the seas. But what of the fourth major land area, Eurasia—the largest single landmass in the world? Covering more than 20 million square miles, this continent extends halfway around the world from the western shores of Portugal to the Siberian Cape Dezhnev. The four major oceans of the world wash the shores of Eurasia.

While this landmass may well be too large to be considered an island, Sir Halford J. MacKinder, a geographer–historian whose works have worldwide acceptance, nevertheless refers to it as the "World Island" whose "heart" is in eastern Europe. Among the most quoted of MacKinder's comments concerning the impact of geography upon the history of the world are the following:

"Who rules East Europe commands the heartland.

"Who rules the heartland commands the World Island.

"Who rules the World Island commands the world."

To this could be added: "Who rules the seas around the World Island rules all."

The state of sea power today is such that not only the World Island, but all of the world can be dominated from the seas. To a degree this has always been true, for civilizations have tended to concentrate upon the peninsulas which protrude from the mother continent of Eurasia. The peninsulas of India and Scandinavia, Kamchatka and Arabia, Iberia and the Balkans, and Europe itself constitute the most striking geographic facts about the huge continent. Ever since Rome and Carthage battled over Italy, peninsulas have been recognized as vulnerable to seaborne flanking attack, such as the one General Douglas MacArthur executed so skillfully at Inchon, Korea. The power that controls the seas around these peninsulas can strike across narrow lands to divide and conquer.

Europe, although it is a multinational subcontinent, is still susceptible to the pressures which may be brought to bear upon a peninsula.

11

The seas left their mark on Europe early in history, for it was these maritime nations that produced the fifteenth- and sixteenth-century explorers who discovered and settled the new worlds of the Americas and traveled to the far reaches of the Eurasian continent and Asia. Only peoples long under maritime influence would have ventured as far as did these great explorers. A primary geographic reason for this is the extremely irregular seacoast which has created some of the finest seaports in the world. There is more coastline per square mile of European landmass than there is on any other continent or subcontinent. Africa, for instance, is three times the size of Europe, but it has a shorter coastline.

The tremendous climatic, political, and commercial influence which the seas have had upon the cradle of Western civilization are offset by another geographic fact. Europe itself is a peninsula, not an island. Had it been an island, its rulers might have concentrated more on the development of their sea power. As it was, the open plains of central Europe, connecting the peninsula to the rest of Eurasia, attracted the immediate concern of western European nations, because there are no natural barriers to any military threat from the east. Thus, with European rulers preoccupied with land armies, England was free to dominate the seas alone.

This dual vulnerability of peninsular Europe to attack by land from the east, and by sea from the north, south, and west, is a crucial factor in today's North Atlantic Treaty Organization defense strategy. In order that NATO's land forces may be prepared to meet any threat across the plains from the east, naval units must control the seas on the other three sides of the great peninsula. Critical to this concept is control of the Mediterranean. Only 550 miles separate the Adriatic and North seas across the neck of the European peninsula. To take full advantage of the southern exposure, major overseas units of the Atlantic Fleet are based in the Mediterranean, from which carrier-based aircraft can extend the influence of sea power to all of Europe.

One other major Eurasian peninsula must be singled out for special consideration. Geographic understanding of Southeast Asia is critical to the security of the free world because political, social,

12

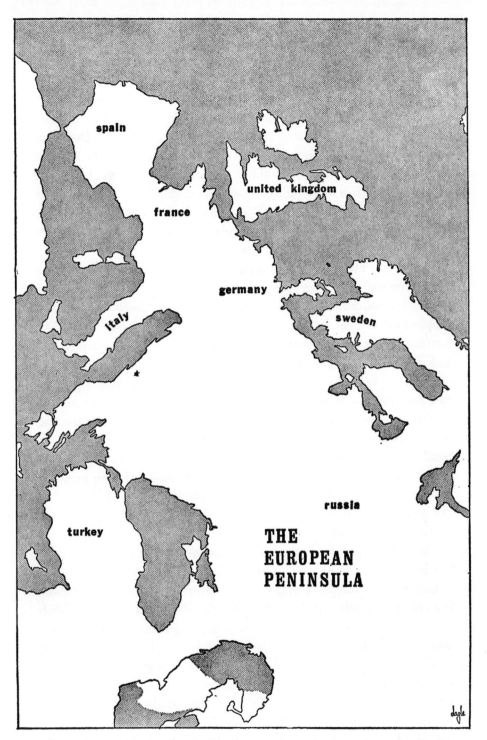

THE EUROPEAN PENINSULA

That Europe is a peninsula has been and continues to be a dominating factor in its political and economic development. The seas have always had a major effect upon Europe, which has more seacoast than all of Africa. World War II amphibious landings were made at Normandy, southern France, Sicily, and Salerno, Italy.

and economic conditions there are very fluid. The Southeast Asian peninsula and an adjacent chain of islands numbering in the thousands form a long, broken horseshoe of land rimming the South China Sea. The peninsular states of Burma, Laos, Vietnam, Thailand, Cambodia, and Malaysia—all areas of conflict—compose the western side of the horseshoe. The three thousand islands of Indonesia descend in a series of stepping-stones toward Australia and then veer north toward the Philippines. The latter chain of more than seven thousand islands forms the eastern side of the horseshoe extending to within three hundred miles of Formosa.

Nature has made Southeast Asia the rice bowl of the Orient. The rice-eating nations of the free world could not survive without access to this region. Southeast Asia has also become the world's major supplier of critical raw materials. Ninety per cent of the world's natural rubber comes from this troubled area. Other forest products and minerals are growing in importance, including kapok and quinine, copra and teak, bauxite and tungsten. Furthermore, Southeast Asia has major iron ore deposits and 65 per cent of the world's tin—all coming from this region so exposed to influence from the sea.

The presence of these raw materials, and the strategic location of Southeast Asia astraddle vital lines of communications and trade, have catapulted young, formerly colonial, nations into the midst of international politics. The transition has been abrupt and disruptive. For some national leaders, the sudden rise to power has been quite heady and intoxicating.

The strife which has accompanied the emergence of these nations has been economic as well as political.

China, the principal architect of the pressures on Southeast Asia, is as poor in agricultural worth as Southeast Asia is rich. The lands of China are simply not capable of producing enough food to maintain more than a minimum standard of living. China is not much larger in area than the United States, but its population is a different story. The latest estimates of the mainland Chinese people number over 670 million, more than three times the population of the United States. Moreover, China has also the fastest-growing population in the world, increasing at a rate of 100 million people each decade.

14

By 1980 there will be twice as many mainland Chinese as there were in 1940 when the crowded nation had difficulty feeding its people. And, within China's own borders, there is little or no hope for any improvement in the food situation.

Not only is China hopelessly lacking in food, but transportation and equipment deficiencies prevent adequate exploitation in areas where there might be some hope of self-sufficiency. Mineral resources, for instance, are tremendous in potential, but the foreseeable future holds no bright prospect for exploitation of their true worth. Naval Academy Professor William W. Jeffries sums up the Chinese plight in this way: "Never in the history of modern times have so many people needed so much to acquire a reasonable degree of self-sufficiency."

This, then, is the most dangerously explosive situation in the world today. As internal pressures mount in China, something will have to give. Because mountainous regions border China on most of its frontiers, expansion overland will be difficult. Thus, sea power could play a decisive role in containing any political or military thrust outward which may be attempted by this boiling nation.

The true giant of Asia, however, is the Soviet Union. Only Texas-style superlatives can be used to describe the vast expanse of this federation of fifteen states which covers a sixth of the earth's land surface. The USSR, three times the size of the United States, stretches east to west through ten time zones.

The Soviet Union is about as self-sufficient as China is not. It raises almost all the food its people need. The natural resources demanded by a modern industrial complex are not only adequate in Russia but they are found in such great supply that reserves are extensive. There are few materials needed for an advanced scientific and technological society which cannot be found somewhere in the 8,700,000 square miles of landmass which make up the Soviet Union.

The Soviet Union, in fact, comes closer to being self-sufficient than any other nation in the world. Yet, as we shall see later, this nation, traditionally a land power, is presently building the world's largest merchant fleet. This new Soviet interest in sea power has taken place

15

in spite of severe geographic limitations facing the USSR. Most of the Soviet Union is situated north of the latitude of Portland, Maine, and its longest coastline faces the ice-clogged Arctic Ocean. Even without the hindrance of ice and foul weather, Soviet ports would be restricted by their geographic relationships to their neighbors. Scandinavian nations overlook the Baltic Sea approaches. Japan controls routes entering Vladivostok. Turkey dominates the Bosporus and Dardanelles access through to the Black Sea.

Why is this self-sufficient land nation turning to the seas? Why is it building military and merchant fleets rivaling those of the free-world maritime leaders? Two of the answers to these questions are geographic in nature.

First, the leaders in the Kremlin realize that even the heartland of the Eurasian continent is vulnerable to the pressures of sea power projected from the north and the south by both conventional and nuclear-armed Polaris-missile forces. With 90 per cent of the rest of the world's populated land areas not more than five hundred miles from the sea, they realize that in the event of hostilities virtually no spot on earth will be beyond the range of attack from the seas. This is the most profound change in the whole history of warfare because sea power can be deployed over three fourths of the earth's surface unhampered by international boundaries. The Soviet Union is determined to take full advantage of this free oceanic "real estate," for it can be used without commitment or obligation by the power that controls the seas.

Secondly, any power that seeks to spread its influence throughout the world must control four bottlenecks of world commerce—the Southeast Asian Strait of Malacca, the Panama Canal, the Suez Canal, and the Straits of Gibraltar.

The peninsular-island chain of Southeast Asia can be a gateway or a barrier to the underside of Asia, depending upon who controls the Strait of Malacca. Sea transport through this narrow channel and other small passages in the island chain is the only link that South Asia has with the rest of the Orient. There are no land routes to the north. Witness the tragic limitations of the now-abandoned Burma Road which forced the Allies to fly over "The Hump" in World War II

16

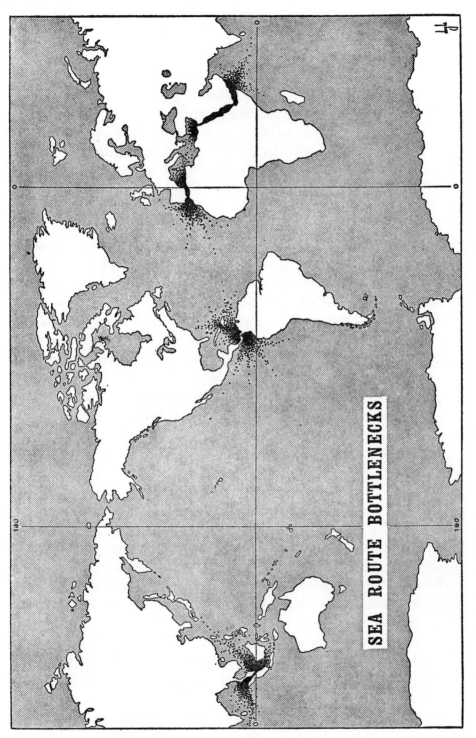

SEA ROUTE BOTTLENECKS

Four "bottlenecks" of the oceanic world—the Strait of Malacca, the Suez Canal, Straits of Gibraltar, and the Panama Canal—are areas of Communist pressure during the cold-war era.

to deliver virtually all of China's war machines and materials, after the Japanese shut the gates of Southeast Asia. China seeks to close these barriers again and thus capture for its exclusive use the rice bowl it needs to feed its hungry millions.

Half a world away, on the doorstep of the United States, the strategic relationship of Cuba to the Panama Canal is easily seen. In the late nineteenth century, Admiral Alfred Mahan warned that completion of the Central American canal would convert the Caribbean into one of the "great highways of the world." He likened the Caribbean trade route to those of the English Channel and the Mediterranean after completion of the Suez Canal. He further warned that the Atlantic–Pacific passage would bring close to United States shores the interests of other nations, friendly and otherwise. A half-century later, the island of Cuba proved his point. Cuba has achieved the unique position of being the western outpost of the Communist colonial empire, at the same time being the headquarters for the United States Navy's Caribbean Sea operations. Cuba stands squarely across the Atlantic access to Panama.

Two other world bottlenecks involve the eastern and western approaches to the Mediterranean Sea, which has played a dramatic commercial and military role in the development of the world. The Straits of Gibraltar have been controlled by Great Britain for two and a half centuries. Today they are threatened by some unrest in northwestern Africa and Spain. The Suez Canal, the Mediterranean-to-Indian-Ocean shortcut used to transport more than 100 billion tons of freight annually, is vital to timely delivery of Middle Eastern oil to Europe and the nations of the free world. Europe could not survive without this oil. The free world could not survive without Europe. At the junction of the Red Sea and the Gulf of Aden, the Soviet Union has built a large seaport for Yemen, a nation in a state of political turmoil and uncertainty.

Peoples of the free-world oceanic alliance and also of the Communist bloc nations, except possibly the Soviet Union, depend upon the trade and free movement of goods along some 70,000 miles of primary sea routes, all of which pass through one of the four bottlenecks. Communist pressures exerted in each of these regions emphasize their importance for survival of the free world or for expansion of the Red empire. Continued probes must be expected. Increasing pressures in these areas, however, will demand an ever-growing Communist reliance upon sea power. This is an inescapable fact of geography. Any land drive outward from eastern Europe or Asia can be outflanked from the seas. To prevent this or to support any leapfrog operation across oceans, control of the seas is a necessity.

It is for this reason that the Soviet Union, occupant of the world's largest single landmass, has not let the glamour of outer space obscure the importance of the oceans. As the Soviet space program captures worldwide attention, that nation is quietly building the world's largest merchant fleet. At the same time, it has become the world's leading undersea power with more commerce-destroying submarines in its fleet than any nation has ever had in war or peace.

The Soviets have studied well their geography and history, including Themistocles, who said hundreds of years before the birth of Christ: "He who commands the sea, has command of everything."

Simply stated, this is the story of sea power in a nutshell.

Ours is an oceanic world. The seven seas have no national identity. Down through the ages, the oceans have remained free to be used by those national powers who had the will and the intelligence to use them for military, economic, social, or political purposes.

The ability of any nation to make the fullest use of the seas depends not only upon its military strength, but also upon the timely exploration of the oceans and their depths. This means the harvesting of the rich mineral, vegetable, and animal resources which the seas hold in store for us, and the use of the waters which cover so much of the world as highways for the transportation of the raw materials and manufactured goods so important to our very economy and our standard of living.

Sea power is total power.

⚓

CHAPTER TWO

"For Want of a Nail . . ."

The United States today is the unchallenged industrial giant of the world. Its dollar is the foundation of the currency and economy of the free world. As a nation, we produce more timesaving consumer goods and our people have more leisure time than anywhere else on earth.

Yet, in many ways, the United States is a "have-not" nation.

We are dependent for our very survival upon raw materials from newly emerging Africa, turbulent Southeast Asia, and restless Latin America. We must have their materials for our strategic defense. Nearly one hundred strategic raw materials consumed in ever-increasing quantities by United States industries are not found on this continent in amounts sufficient to satisfy our production appetites.

These materials range from A to Z—antimony to zircon.

Antimony is required to harden metals for antifriction bearings, cable sheathings, and ammunition. Few Americans remember how to crank a Model T Ford, but they would have to learn if our foreign supplies of antimony were cut off. There would be no storage batteries to turn over automobile starters. The United States imports 87 per cent of antimony for its industrial needs.

Amosite asbestos does not exist in the Western Hemisphere. It must be imported from the Union of South Africa if we are to have steam-resistant insulation for turbines.

Bauxite is imported in enormous tonnages from Caribbean countries and from the northeastern Latin American nations of Surinam and British Guiana. Four pounds of bauxite are used to produce one pound of aluminum. A shortage of aluminum would halt aircraft and missile production. Aluminum consumer goods from teakettles to house siding would be missing from store shelves if the supply of bauxite were cut off. Eighty-nine per cent of our bauxite comes to our shores by way of the sea.

Beryllium is used principally as an alloying element with copper to produce a tough, hard alloy which has great resistance to fatigue and shock and which does not lose its hardness at high temperatures. Springs, diaphragms, bearings, and bushings are produced from corrosion-resistant beryllium for use in aircraft and missile construction. Other uses requiring beryllium alloys are nonsparking safety tools, spot-welding electrodes, and high-stress castings. Unalloyed beryllium is used in nuclear reactors, cyclotrons, spacecraft, and X-ray windows. Ninety-seven per cent of the beryllium used in this country is produced from ore imported by ship, mostly from Latin America, Africa, and India.

Chromium, derived from chromite, is essential to alloys used in jet engines, gas turbines, gun barrels, ammunition, and armor plate. It is added to stainless steel to combat corrosion, wear, and heat effects. No substitute will produce the same results. One hundred per cent of the chromite used in this country is imported, largely from the Philippines and Africa.

Cobalt is demanded for high-temperature, magnetic, and hard-facing alloys for jet and gas turbine engines; high-speed tool steels; paint and enamel driers. Substitutes are not acceptable. All the cobalt we need is imported, mostly from Belgium and the Congo.

Coffee may not be a necessity, but for those who cannot get started in the morning without it, little need be said other than the fact that every single bean reaches our shores in a ship.

Columbite is the principal ore from which columbium and tantalum are derived. Columbium is required for construction of nuclear reactors and also as a carbide stabilizer for stainless steel for boilers and refinery equipment. It imparts superior fatigue strength to alloys employed in jet engines, gas turbines, rockets, and missiles. Tantalum is used in electronics manufacturing. There is no adequate substitute. Without tantalum, we would be unable to produce television or transistors of any type. Yet none of the basic ore, columbite, is

21

produced domestically. Malaya, Brazil, Nigeria, the Congo, and Mozambique provide much of the raw material used by American industry.

Copper deposits in this country satisfy much of our domestic industrial needs for this exceptional conductor of electricity. However, curtailment of imports of copper still would cripple the electrical industry of this nation and the homes, businesses, and commerce which it serves. Copper shortages would also eliminate the manufacture of brass and bronze. Imports are largely from Chile and Canada.

Hard fibers such as Manila, sisal, and henequen are used for manufacture of most of the nation's rope, hawsers, drilling cable, binder and baler twine. None of these fibers are grown in the United States. Most are imported by ship and the flow must be constant, for stockpiling of natural fibers is restricted due to their deterioration in storage.

The United States is dependent on ocean-borne imports of lead because it produces only slightly more than a third of what its industry needs. Ships, automobiles, and rail passenger and freight cars require lead for batteries and bearings. Lead is one of the most useful metals in the chemical industry. It is an effective radiation shield and an essential ingredient of gasoline additives. A shortage of lead would cripple the production of batteries and ammunition.

Manganese is essential as a reducing agent and cleanser in the manufacture of steel. Without manganese, we would have no alternative but to shut down our steel mills. Ninety-nine per cent of the United States' requirements is imported by ship from Latin America, Africa, and India.

Mica, a mineral, is the principal rigid insulating material used in the manufacture of electrical and electronic equipment. The lack of sheet mica products could seriously cripple electronic production and retard military operations which have become so dependent upon electronics. Ninety-seven per cent of the mica consumed in this country comes from overseas, largely from India.

Sugar is "critical" to many coffee and soft-drink enthusiasts.

Nationwide, Americans consume ninety-seven pounds of sugar per capita each year. Two of every three pounds is imported by ship.

Thorium is used increasingly in alloys requiring high temperature applications. Thorium oxide's melting point is 3,220 degrees Centigrade. It complements uranium as a source of energy in nuclear reactors and also is used in high quality optics. Ninety-three per cent of that consumed in this country is imported, mostly from South Africa.

Tin is a basic element for production of everything from cans to engine bearings, upon which latter item most of our transportation equipment is dependent. This nation's only tin mine, located in Alaska, closed down in 1955. Southeast Asia and Bolivia are our present sources of supply.

At the bottom of the alphabet is zircon, which is critically important to our nuclear submarine program, and to the construction of all nuclear power plants. In 1945, the United States imported twenty-one pounds of zircon. In 1958, this nation imported two and a half million pounds of this mineral. One hundred per cent of our supply is imported by sea transport, and it comes mostly from Australia.

Among the many, many other commodities which this nation imports in sizable quantities are iron, nickel, petroleum, tungsten, uranium, vegetable oils, and zinc. It should be noted that most of the imports upon which the United States is dependent are minerals. The United States consumes more than half of *all* the minerals produced in the free world!

In short, airplanes would not fly, trains would not run, automobiles would be stalled, electric lights would not burn, television sets would be dark, radios would be silent, and most of our timesaving gadgets in the home would be missing if it were not for the raw materials which we must import day after day. Most important of all, our Army, Navy, and Air Force would be incapable of defense of this nation.

If we need these imports so badly, can we not go out and purchase them on the world market? Yes, but we must also have something to offer besides gold dollars. No individual, business, industry, or nation can buy and buy and buy without also selling other things to balance the books. The supply of dollars is not without limits. A nation can draw upon gold reserves only so long. Either we must trade or fade.

An example of trade would be a dairy farmer and a shoemaker bartering milk for shoes; but actually, trade is much more complex than this. States within our own nation trade. Iowa raises corn and hogs. Massachusetts makes shoes. Texas raises cattle. California builds electronic equipment. Florida raises citrus fruits. Michigan builds automobiles. Washington harvests timber and Wisconsin brews beer. The agriculture and the industry of each region produces that for which climate, soil, water, natural resources, and the labor supply best suit it. Each region then sells its goods in order to buy products which it does not produce.

For the same reason that states trade among themselves, nations must trade with each other. While it has only 6 per cent of the world's population, the United States still produces more than one third of the world's manufactured industrial goods. This production must be maintained at a high level so that the economy of the United States can continue to expand—as it must—to provide jobs for the thousands upon thousands who enter the labor market for the first time each year. These are primarily young men and women completing their formal education with varying degrees of training and skills.

An expanding economy also demands that production be greatly increased each year. Because domestic markets tend to be unlimited, we must turn to world markets for the sale of these manufactured goods. We must also sell much of our agricultural production on world markets. America is the breadbasket of the world. A very large percentage of the billion-bushel annual United States wheat crop is shipped overseas into foreign markets. The United States also ships substantial quantities of rice to the Orient. Cotton, feed grains, soybeans, corn, and tobacco—all are major agricultural exports.

Between industrial and agricultural exports, this nation's sales overseas total some 25 billion dollars annually. If we are to maintain our balance of trade, however, we must increase our exports by about 1 billion dollars annually. That this can be done has been proven in our trade with Africa. At one time, the United States' trade with African nations consisted only of imports of raw materials. Today, however, markets for manufactured goods have been expanded so that our exports to Africa exceed our imports by 33 per cent. Yankee ingenuity has been and must continue to be used to develop foreign markets for our industrial goods. An American firm, for instance, recently showed an electronic peanut-sorting device at a Japanese trade fair. Imagination resulted in sales. The machine is now in use in the Far East, sorting not peanuts, but pearls.

Capitalizing fully on the opportunities offered by foreign markets will achieve for this country full employment, and economic and industrial growth. Three million jobs in the United States are attributable directly to the export business. The United States can expand this even more by helping nonindustrial nations through their own industrial revolutions. This will increase the demand for American know-how and American manufactured goods and industrial supplies. Thus the economies of all nations will grow through increased world trade. It happened within the United States during the last century. It can happen in the world community in the next century.

Trade, of course, requires movement of goods. The only practical method of transporting large volumes of goods across the oceans of the world is in ships.

It is a known fact that a ton of merchandise may be moved in a cargo ship for only a fraction of what it would cost by air transport. If we are going to trade with the rest of the world, we must utilize merchant ships.

But—whose ships?

For the most part, the United States now ships its exports and imports in ships flying foreign flags. Ninety per cent of our international trade is moving in cargo vessels registered in nations other than the United States.

Is this contrary to the national interests of the United States? National policy says "Absolutely!" Historically, the spoken policy of this nation has always called for the maintenance of a strong,

COMPARATIVE CARGO RATES

TYPE OF CARGO	FROM	TO	Via Ship Cost per long ton (2240 pounds) or 40 cubic feet	Via Air Cost per long ton (2240 pounds)
Aircraft Engines	New York	London	$50.00	$ 537.60
Automobiles (boxed)	New York	Capetown	31.25	4,054.40
Machinery	Baltimore	Sydney	65.00	4,368.00
Petroleum Products	New York	Dar-es-Salaam	30.50	3,136.00
Foodstuffs	Boston	Rio de Janeiro	68.50 + 7.00 surcharge	1,500.80
Machinery	New Orleans	Bremen	36.25	869.12
Perfumes	Paris	New York	102 per cu. met.	440.00
Scotch Whiskey	Glasgow	Norfolk	33.75	470.40
Sewing Machines	New Orleans	Santos	62.50	1,590.40
Household Refrigerators	Mobile	Dakar	39.25	3,427.20
Fur Pelts	Hamburg	New York	89 per cu. met.	509.20
Canned Goods	San Francisco	Tokyo	55.50 p. 2000 lb.	2,000.00
Trucks or Trailers	Seattle	Yokohama	52.25 "	Can't handle
Drugs	New York	Cristobal	55.00	739.20
Electrical Equipment	Portland, Oregon	Tokyo	61.75 "	2,000.00
Telescopes	Kobe	Seattle	35.50 "	1,500.00
Transistor Radios	Yokohama	San Francisco	33.25 "	1,500.00

American-based merchant fleet. As far back as 1641, the Colony of Massachusetts went on record in support of this cause. George Washington, Thomas Jefferson, Abraham Lincoln, Theodore Roosevelt, Herbert Hoover, Franklin D. Roosevelt, and John F. Kennedy—all of these leaders believed that a strong merchant marine was in the best interests of the United States. President Lyndon B. Johnson declared that "a strong merchant marine is a guarantee of national and economic stability."

As an integral part of our economy, the merchant marine employs about 200,000 people. It generates $1,500,000,000 of our gross national product each year. The decline of any industry of such huge proportions would be cause for concern. The impact of the merchant shipping industry is not only of major importance to our national economy, but it is completely enmeshed in the complex monetary exchange and gold reserve situation. Only a small fraction of the total costs of hauling our imports and exports to and from American shores goes to United States shipping firms. The balance goes into the treasuries of foreign companies and nations and thus becomes a deficit in our balance of payments. If there were no American-flag vessels plying the shipping routes of the world, the situation would be even blacker than it is at present. The presence of the United States industry in the shipping markets of the world has a stabilizing effect upon freight rates charged United States businessmen exporting and importing.

If our own merchant marine were allowed to wither and die completely and if the United States were to become dependent upon foreign nations to haul this nation's goods, shipping rates would soar astronomically. This, in fact, happened early in World War I and freight rates increased as much as 1,000 per cent. Should our merchant marine completely disappear, the resulting prohibitive freight rates could strangle this nation. Economically, the need for a strong, healthy merchant marine is tremendous.

Politically, the need is just as great, although it may be less apparent than the cold talk of hard cash. There was a time when the United States could relax in a political "fortress America" attitude, but that day is gone—never to return. The United States has been swept into a race between two diametrically opposing philosophies— democracy and communism. The goal is the economic resources and markets of the world. That is what the cold war of the mid-century is all about. To take the fullest possible political advantage of its economic efforts, through both commercial and foreign aid, American goods must move in American ships sailed by American sailors under the American flag. Hondurans, say, manning United States-owned ships camouflaged with foreign flags of convenience, do nothing to further understanding among the peoples of the world of the American way of life. American materials and commodities sent to struggling new nations through a multi-billion-dollar foreign aid program lose much of their political punch if they are unloaded from a ship flying, for example, a Liberian flag. To capture the full impact of the greatness of America, the United States merchant fleet as well as its military vessels must be seen throughout the world.

Militarily, it is impossible to move and maintain a large body of troops anywhere overseas without sea power to supply them. Considerable progress has been made in airlifting troops to trouble spots throughout the world, but when they arrive they must be married to pre-positioned heavy equipment and supplies which have been sea-lifted in advance. Air transport cannot move the heavy equipment demanded by a modern army, nor can it maintain an overseas force which consumes tremendous volumes of materials and supplies. In this respect, Korean War statistics speak for themselves. Every soldier landed in Korea was accompanied by five tons of equipment. It required the daily delivery of 64 pounds of supplies to keep him there. Fifty-four million tons of dry cargo and 22 million tons of petroleum products were hauled to Korea by ships. For every ton of transpacific airfreight, 270 tons of sea freight were moved to Korea. For every ton of airfreight carried across the Pacific, four tons of aviation gasoline were delivered across the Pacific by ship. And, in the Korean War, six out of every seven men went there by ship. Thus, to maintain an army overseas, sea transport will be needed for the foreseeable future.

Merchant shipping could also play a critical recovery role in the event of nuclear attack. Coastal sea transport, easily cleansed of contaminating radioactive fallout, could be the first mode of transportation to recover from such an attack.

It is ironic that the capacity of the American merchant marine to carry goods across the oceans should decrease at precisely the time when our exports and imports are achieving record levels. Exports have increased 85 per cent during the past decade. Imports have increased 70 per cent in the same period.

By contrast, the Soviet Union is building the most modern merchant fleet in the world, and it is expanding at a rate far exceeding that of any other nation. The competitive threat of the Russian merchant fleet is so strong that a former Secretary of the Navy recently warned that the day may not be too far off when the United States may have to ask Communist state-owned Soviet ships to carry to the United States our purchases of strategic raw materials for the defense of our nation and for our effort in the space race.

Apathy on the part of the public who do not know or do not care about the need for a strong, vital merchant fleet has permitted this condition to develop. The public has failed to understand that the merchant ship, seen only by those on our coasts and only then, until it is hull-down on the horizon, is just as important to the economic existence of this nation as is the freight train which bellows its way through town at two o'clock every night.

An old nursery rhyme goes this way: "For want of a nail, the shoe was lost. For want of a shoe, the horse was lost . . ." and so on until a whole kingdom was finally lost. Is the unromantic, but essential, merchant ship the "nail" in the rhyme as far as the United States is concerned?

⚓

CHAPTER THREE

Sea Power's Role in the
Political Development of the United States

Hindsight is twenty-twenty.

This is how some present-day philosophers express the sentiments of William Shakespeare, whose brief comment on the impact of history—"What is past is prologue"—is inscribed upon the walls of the National Archives building in Washington, D.C.

From whichever generation one looks at history, the same truth is revealed: From history comes an explanation of today's events and guidance for a course of action for tomorrow.

Sea power is no exception to this rule, although it was not until late in the nineteenth century that an American naval officer made clear the impact of sea power upon history. Captain Alfred Mahan was lecturing at the newly established Naval War College at about the same time that the United States Navy was completing the transition from sail to steam.

Seeking guidance for this trying period, when most Americans were looking inward and westward, Mahan turned to the oceans that surrounded this land of ours. He studied the nautical history of two centuries earlier, tracing the political growth and transition of European nations beginning in 1660. This was when Charles II sat upon the throne of England and bluntly told Louis XIV of France that, "It is the custom of the English to command at sea."

During the next 123 years of juggling alliances, the one constant factor was the steady growth of British sea power. Holland was a major maritime nation when William of Orange ascended to the thrones of both England and Holland, but William promptly subjected the strong Dutch navy to the control of the admirals of England. This was a political action which ultimately stripped Holland of her military capability of protecting her then-sizable merchant fleets.

While the ruling classes of Portugal and Spain scorned the British as a "nation of shopkeepers," the English succeeded in destroying Iberian fleets whenever they could catch them out of port. Ultimately, British sea power deprived Spain and Portugal of access to American and African gold, silver, and gems, upon which these two nations largely existed. The result was that these Iberian empires began to decline. Later, Napoleon Bonaparte, who never was able to understand the importance of the oceans, "preserved" his fleets by not allowing them to engage the enemy. Ships caught by the British were destroyed. Those that escaped rotted away in port. Eventually, through his neglect of the complementary arm of sea power, Napoleon fell.

By contrast, the British Empire, built upon the foundations of its traditional sea power, continued to prosper, grow, and thrive. The political atmosphere in this island nation demanded an active navy sufficiently large and strong to protect an aggressive British commercial fleet which ranged throughout the world. This, in turn, gave the British the military and economic vehicles with which to impose their political wills upon peoples and governments of most of the world, from Lisbon to the Orient. The result was "Pax Britannica" which lasted through much of the late eighteenth century and the nineteenth century. Thus, this "nation of shopkeepers" dominated the world, due to its understanding of the oceans and the effective and efficient use of sea power.

Mahan taught that national sea power is a politico-military force composed of naval and commercial fleets capable of transiting the oceans of the world at will, served by overseas bases strategically located throughout the world, and exploiting worldwide markets and sources of raw materials to the fullest possible extent.

Although the period about which Admiral Mahan wrote was one of sail, he related history so well to the steam-powered genera-

31

tion in which he lived that the world accepted his thesis of sea power as a traditional vehicle of political power. Today, we are in the midst of another transition—that of converting from oil to the atom. Still, the same truths will remain valid in a fully nuclear-powered age. In fact, the impact of such nuclear sea power will be greater than ever before, because nuclear-powered ships are not shackled by the need to refuel every few days, but can sail as long as provisions and manpower will permit. Moreover, nuclear power has produced speeds and endurance capabilities formerly undreamed of in the mid-twentieth century.

Military sea power is composed of self-contained communities of fighting men able to move unhindered over three quarters of the earth's surface. Fighting ships can be completely unfettered by political treaties, base rights, or expensive overseas facilities. When their right to move in international waters is challenged, as was the case in the Tonkin Gulf in 1964, the response can be measured, controlled, and deliberate. Graduated response to fit any political situation is the keystone of military sea power.

Admiral Mahan recounted the role of sea power, both military and commercial, in the development of England to show the impact of this political force upon the growth of a nation in the period before the American Revolution. In the scant two hundred years since the United States became a nation, sea power has continued to play an invaluable and decisive role in our national development. The stage for American independence was set by an economy drive launched by King George of England. In addition to underestimating the determination of the colonies to win greater freedom and self-rule, George deviated from a long-standing British policy of maintaining a fleet equal to the combined navies of France and Spain. The result was that British fleets were spread too thinly at a time critical to American independence. The political rivalries of Europe exerted an additional influence upon the ultimate success of the Revolution. France, Spain, and Holland all envied British sea power and constantly sought ways to weaken it even more than King George did in the name of economy. Ultimately, each declared war upon England, forcing even greater dissipation of British naval strength—which of course proved of immeasurable value to the Americans.

Benedict Arnold was among the first Americans to use sea power successfully for national defense. In 1776, the British drove down Lake Champlain from Canada in an attempt to invade the colonies and isolate New England from the southern states. General Arnold, who had been a merchant sailor in civilian life, hastily built a small, ragtag collection of ships with which he succeeded in slowing the British drive until winter. Nature joined the side of the Yankees in delaying for a year the efforts of the British to divide and conquer the fledgling nation.* In that crucial year of the Revolution, the colonies united and became strong enough to prevent further invasion from the north. Ultimately, with the valuable assistance of French sea power, independence was attained.

Less than a score of years after American independence, France and the United States, formerly allies, were at odds because of politics and sea power. A British-American treaty of 1796, imposed upon the United States largely because of the force of British sea power, permitted British seizure of French cargoes carried in American merchant ships. Three years of undeclared "quasi war" followed between France and the United States. The basic issue in dispute concerned the free movement of commercial shipping—an issue which escalated into hot war a few years later.

But political winds shift constantly. A decade after the French-American dispute, the United States again found itself engaged in a war with England. With stunning victories in the War of 1812, the American Navy came of age. From that time forward, the Navy has served as an essential vehicle for extension of the foreign policies of the United States.

During these early years, the domestic policies of our neighbors also played a part in the growth of the United States Navy. In the struggle of South American nations to achieve independence from Spain and Portugal (both weakened through neglect of their own

---

* One of Arnold's fleet, the galley *Philadelphia,* is now on exhibit at the Smithsonian Institution, Washington, D.C.

sea power), these emerging nations chartered privateers to prey upon merchant ships of the colonial powers. The crews, who were little more than pirates, were none too careful about distinguishing among the flags flown by their victims. When the Stars and Stripes came under attack, a strong United States Caribbean squadron was formed to protect American merchant shipping from this indiscriminate plunder. The creation of this naval force permitted the proclaiming of the Monroe Doctrine that European powers would have to stay out of domestic politics in the Western Hemisphere. The United States Navy was then, and is now, the vehicle for enforcing this policy.

In the Civil War, sea power, though not spectacular, was at least decisive. Union control of the sea-lanes around the Southern states and the Federal Navy's ability to use major rivers of the South, including the Mississippi, eventually strangled the Confederacy. This unyielding Union blockade, with its constantly increasing pressure, was the principal naval strategy of the Union. It worked with capital success. Not possessing heavy industry and unable to consistently break through the blockade, the Confederacy's days were numbered.

With the exception of the Civil War, the last half of the nineteenth century found the United States Navy playing its least expensive but one of its most effective roles in international politics—showing the flag. Increasing overseas trade began to stir interest in the Far East. In the quest for new markets and sources of raw materials, the United States turned its eyes toward Japan, whose ports had previously been closed to all foreign ships. A naval squadron under the command of Commodore Matthew Calbraith Perry was sent to establish Japanese-American relations. Commodore Perry's mission was eminently successful. Trade commenced not only between the United States and Japan, but also between that Asian nation and France and England. Later, Navy Commander Robert W. Shufeldt, sent to Korea after American merchant sailors had been captured and murdered there, succeeded in negotiating a treaty with that peninsular country, bringing it out of isolation and into the family of trading nations.

When Spanish-American relations became tense in 1898, the USS *Maine* was sent to Cuba on a "show-the-flag" mission to display the muscle behind our policies. The still-mysterious sinking of the *Maine* in Havana Harbor precipitated war. "Remember the Maine" was the battle cry.

Victory in the Spanish-American War provided the United States with the far-flung bases in the Atlantic and Pacific which were then, and are now, vital elements of true sea power.

Together with these developments involving our own Navy, a realignment of naval power in the western Pacific was to prove of great significance to the United States, although its importance may not have been recognized at the time. In 1894 there had been a war between Japan and China, commencing with a massive naval action off the Yalu River. It ended with the Japanese capture of Port Arthur. Thus, only forty years after having been brought into the family of nations by Commodore Perry, Japan began its ascendency as a major naval power in the Pacific. One day she would challenge the combined might of the United States and Britain. At the time, however, China was the only Asiatic nation that could have kept Japan in check, but she had allowed her fleets to decay, and thus abdicated her influence as a maritime nation after the Yalu defeat. Before World War II, Japan's naval power was challenged only once—by Russia.

In February 1904, Japanese torpedo boats steamed boldly into Port Arthur to attack the Russian navy in its home port. Thus started the decline of Russia's naval influence in the Pacific. In May, 1905, the rout was completed when the battle fleets of the two nations met in the Strait of Tsushima. The smaller Russian fleet, which had exhausted itself after sailing halfway around the world via the Atlantic and Indian oceans, was paralyzed by the accuracy of Japanese gunfire. Only two Russian destroyers and a cruiser escaped to limp on to safety at Vladivostok. One hundred years after the Battle of Trafalgar in 1805, Admiral Heihachiro Togo won a victory as significant as that of Lord Horatio Nelson's. After Tsushima, Japan became one of the great naval powers of the world, embarking upon a program of naval expansion with which it projected its political and economic ambitions during the next forty years.

Meanwhile, the United States Navy was making its own presence felt on the international scene. Captain B. H. McCalla of the USS *Newark*, on China station in 1900, was influential in obtaining the cooperation of the British, Austrians, Japanese, and Italians to quell the Boxer Rebellion. In 1912, a United States force restored order in Nicaragua and two years later the capture of Veracruz by naval landing forces led to the fall of a Mexican government which had achieved its rule by intrigue and assassination. A constitutional government followed.

World Wars I and II proved conclusively the military aspects of Mahan's thesis on the importance of sea power and its interrelationship with political strength.

As World War I commenced in Europe, between the Allied and Central Powers, the United States was selling—directly and indirectly—great quantities of supplies and munitions to both sides. Each of the belligerents tried to shut off United States trade with its enemy through enforcement of naval blockades. The superior British surface navy was far more effective. As England's blockade of the Continent became tighter and tighter, Germany was deprived of American materials, and the Kaiser's undersea fleet turned to all-out indiscriminate submarine warfare in a last-ditch effort to strangle England. This was a calculated German politico-military risk that the United States would not fight her, or if it did, it could not be effective before the submarine blockade starved the British Isles into submission.

But Kaiser Wilhelm's crystal ball proved to be cloudy. His underestimation of American industrial and military ability plus Yankee determination was fatal to his empire. The Americans responded quickly and effectively, with the United States Navy reviving a centuries-old military defense against commerce raiders, the convoy, to shepherd troops and supplies across the Atlantic to win victory in Europe.

After World War I, U.S. politics influenced American sea power more than sea power influenced U.S. politics. Navy strategists believed that this country had to maintain a strong naval posture or else accept a second-rate position as a world power. Accordingly, they set out to build the world's largest fleet with which to maintain freedom of the seas and ensure peace and security through oceanic strength—much as the British had done in the previous century. This, of course, would have meant surpassing the British in naval power. A strange political coalition of isolationists and Anglophiles prevented this by pressing for the arms limitation treaties of the 1920's. These restricted the major powers in numbers and size of warships, placing the United States and Britain on a parity basis. As for Japan, she was permitted a navy smaller than those of the two major powers, but larger than those of third-rate France and Italy. Despite this relegation to second-rate status, Japan benefited more from the treaties than any other nation.

As an inducement for Japanese support of the treaties, Great Britain and the United States agreed not to further fortify any outposts in the Pacific; and Japan was permitted to annex all of defeated Germany's Pacific island possessions. This agreement ended a Japanese-American naval arms race which we could have won handily with our vastly superior industrial might. Thus, the stage was set for the Pearl Harbor attack in 1941.

In the twenties, the United States led the way in voluntary scrapping of its Navy. This naturally delayed the much needed expansion and modernization of the American Navy for nearly a decade and a half. Even in the mid-thirties, when the United States once again began to rebuild its fleets, it did so within the confines of an agreement to maintain parity with the British navy.

Japan, meanwhile, leaped to a head start on naval construction, unshackled by any unilateral restrictions after once casting aside formal treaty limitations. Its rapidly growing fleet became an essential weapon for consolidation of its "Greater East Asia Co-Prosperity Sphere," which in nonpropaganda terms merely meant the engulfment of all East Asia by Japan. This goal could be achieved only through control of the western Pacific, including the waters of Southeast Asia.

Conquest-oriented Japan believed that if it knocked out the United States Fleet in the Pacific it could proceed without interference to capture the Philippine Islands and the Dutch East Indies with their wealth of oil, rubber, and tin. With these possessions consolidated,

Japan then could isolate Australia and New Zealand through capture and control of the South Pacific islands. Finally the ultimate goal could be achieved—subjugation of all mainland China. This was a strategy built around a powerful, modern navy and dependent upon continued political division and bickering within the United States as to whether or not to become embroiled in war.

The attack upon Pearl Harbor sealed the doom of Japanese aggressive dreams. In spite of early successes in the western Pacific, the Japanese could not match the industrial and military might of the United States, whose aroused populace immediately united for a single cause—the total defeat of the Japanese empire and its Axis allies.

Never in the history of mankind has a war been so total, so all-inclusive as was World War II. It was fought in virtually every corner of the earth. Every element of political and military warfare known to mankind was brought into play during its four years. Many innovations were made in the art of war. Most of the aircraft the Navy used to cover advancing ships across the Pacific were only on the drawing boards when war broke out. Most of the myriad of special ships which the Navy developed to carry and deposit invasion forces on hostile beaches were not even on the drawing boards in 1941. Generally speaking, the weapons and tactics used to achieve final victory in 1945 were not even dreamed of half a decade earlier.

Even as the military effort reached its climax, the Allies were looking ahead to the political problems of a war-torn world, and anticipating the responsibilities which would follow victory. United States administrators were prepared to serve occupational governments, and statesmen met to create in the United Nations a world body which would be able to grant the world permanent peace through cooperation and understanding.

Victory catapulted the United States into an unsought role as political, economic, and military leader of the free world, but some were not prepared to accept this mantle. After World War II, domestic politics once again dominated the scene and almost destroyed American sea power. Relying too heavily on dreams of world peace, the United States succumbed to the political cry of "Get the boys home!"

Within days after the Japanese surrender, American ships were stripped of substantial portions of their manpower. So complete was the manpower reduction that some ships in the United States occupation fleets anchored in Tokyo Bay could have fought only a few minutes before the flow of ammunition from the magazines to the guns would have halted.

When the Korean War broke out, the Navy was still shorthanded and lacking in many types of ships. All our eggs had been put in one basket—that is, the "more bang for the buck" concept of an all-out nuclear deterrent deliverable only by a strategic air force. The nation was ill-equipped to fight a conventional war. One of the most dramatic commentaries of the nation's sea power shortcomings was revealed at the landings at Wonsan. Although the forces defending the Korean beach were relatively few, the invasion was halted for eight costly days. One of the most elementary of naval defenses, mines, which had been laid by coolies sailing in sampans—vessels of a type in use before the birth of Christ—had completely halted a twentieth-century invasion force of the world's most powerful nation.

As the total potential destructiveness of a nuclear exchange increases, the pendulum appears to be swinging back toward more limited conflicts—restricted as to types and numbers of weapons, men committed, and regions of involvement, such as the war in Vietnam. More and more, conventional warfare has reentered the strategic thinking of both the free world and the Communist world. The Soviet Union, which is the only major nautical power opposing the United States, appears to envision a naval war of blockade and commerce destruction as a most probable type of war in the future. This is made evident by the Soviet's building lighter coastal ships of cruiser and destroyer size, and by the tremendous emphasis the Red Navy is placing upon submarines. The Soviets maintain a fleet of about 450 submarines, and they are constantly updating and modernizing those in their inventory through addition of newer, longer-range, nuclear boats.

The emphasis placed by the Soviets upon commerce-destroying warships, both surface and subsurface, also increases the possibility that any major confrontation between the Soviet Union and the

United States could be a war limited to ocean areas rather than the all-out, totally destructive nuclear exchange more often envisioned by Americans. Conceivably, such a war could be fought entirely between navies, without any land areas being involved. It could be a logical extension of the current cold-war economic competition in which we and the Soviets are now engaged. However, such a war will not be fought if the Soviet Union can achieve its goal of world economic domination through continued expansion and wise utilization of its already formidable merchant fleet.

Even if worldwide sea war never materialized, regional conflicts will involve maritime strategies, for these encounters of East and West have already occurred. And they will probably continue to happen on the fringes of the power centers of the world—in places such as Korea, Formosa, India, Aden, Cyprus, Africa, Lebanon, Latin America, Cuba, the Arctic, Vietnam, and other areas on the Southeast Asian peninsula.

Whether the conflict be regional or general, the missions of the United States Navy will remain the same as they have always been. In wartime, the Navy must maintain freedom of the seas by being able to destroy opposing naval forces, by being the advance force for any invasion, by moving troops and supplies across the seas, by destroying the enemy's merchant fleets and thereby destroying his industrial capacity to fight. In peacetime, the Navy must also guarantee freedom of the seas to permit the free-world movement of merchant ships competing in the race for world trade and markets.

With the ability to range free and uninhibited over 75 per cent of the earth's surface, the Navy can reach virtually all areas of the world to extend the impact of sea power wherever and whenever trouble occurs. Thus, the Navy must have the instantaneous capability to respond to any crisis, military or political. The presence of a naval force capable of any variety of responses, from merely waiting on the scene to fighting any type of war, can exert a great amount of political pressure in international relations. An outstanding example of this was the Cuban quarantine. Without firing a shot, the Navy put down a calculated gamble which could have completely changed the balance of military power in the world. The gamble failed because of the determined presence of the United States Navy, obviously ready for action and backed up by a people willing to accept even the risk of general war in order to prevent the establishment of a nuclear missile capability in Cuba—a force which could have been used only for atomic blackmail.

Almost a century ago, Admiral Mahan taught that effective sea power depends upon geography, commerce, industry, foreign markets, overseas bases, and a people conscious of the value of sea power. People who have recognized these elements of sea power have used them to advantage to become world leaders. Nations who have failed to appreciate the influence of sea power upon the political, social, and economic course of history have been swallowed up in the forward march of civilization.

Mahan's thesis remains valid today. Militarily, industrially, economically, we are dependent upon the seas. Throughout history, the presence or absence of a strong fleet has had an important bearing upon the political development of the nation and the conduct of its international affairs.

The oceanic alliances in which we are involved today demand that the role of sea power be substantial and decisive for the foreseeable future if we are going to meet the responsibilities of free-world leadership which have been thrust upon us.

⚓

CHAPTER FOUR

Our Oceanic Alliances

When George Washington left the Presidency, he warned Congress that the United States should not become involved in foreign entanglements. Washington's comments may have been appropriate for his day, although it should be remembered that foreign "entanglements" helped substantially in achieving our independence. But what Washington could never have envisioned was the kind of world in which this generation lives—a world in which science and technology have brought people so close together that, without leaving their American living rooms, they can see the Olympic games in Japan or watch a French vaudeville show.

We can travel from San Francisco to Chicago in an hour or so. We can orbit the world in ninety minutes. We could destroy the world in an estimated fifteen minutes. Unless we are able to truly understand our neighbors and work closely with those who want to maintain their freedom, this last possibility could happen here all too easily. Prevention of nuclear war is a matter of elementary survival.

There are two ways that atomic destruction can be avoided. One, which surprisingly has some advocates in this country, would be to abolish one's armed forces regardless of what any other nation might do. This would let the world know that this nation would not resist aggression. A nation following such a course of action could only expect to submit to the most aggressive power remaining in the world. This would be the peace and security of slavery.

The alternative is building a strong and collective defense system that will serve to convince any would-be aggressor that the odds would be too great to embark upon any reckless nuclear adventure.

This difficult course of action takes tremendous quantities of money, manpower, and hardware. The wisdom of Solomon is needed to determine the exact amount of men and materials required. Too much is wasteful. Too little is suicide.

In building such a defense, the United States has found it physically and financially impossible to "go it alone." No nation in the free world is capable of meeting the imperialistic thrusts of the Communist empire by itself. The only alternative is alliance. Conditions have so changed in the two centuries since Washington led us to independence that the United States is now involved in the military defense and economic support of more than sixty nations of the free world. NATO, CENTO, SEATO, RIO, ANZUS—all are common terms in our diplomatic vocabulary. A glance at the geography of these multilateral alliances and our bilateral mutual defense pacts with the Philippines, Japan, South Korea, and Formosa quickly reveals one common denominator. They all involve oceanic nations linked together by the sea-lanes of trade and commerce.

The Southeast Asia Treaty Organization, SEATO, created to achieve collective security in Southeast Asia and the southwestern Pacific, is composed of eight nations with broadly differing historical, economic, and political backgrounds: Australia, France, New Zealand, Pakistan, the Philippines, Thailand, the United Kingdom, and the United States. Although initially united for a single purpose, that of collective security, these nations soon found that their mutual confidence carried them into cooperative ventures outside the fields of defense. Constant consultation concerning economic, social, and cultural development helps to raise standards of living, health, and education for all the peoples of the region.

These same goals are spelled out in the charter under which the Central Treaty Organization was created. Iran, Pakistan, Turkey, the United Kingdom, and the United States joined to promote their economic well-being and to bring about closer friendship, cooperation, and understanding, as well as to build roads and railways to link member nations with seaports in order to provide improved access to CENTO nations and to provide these mid-Eastern areas with a focal point for world trade. Militarily, CENTO is principally an

43

oceanic alliance, as is shown by the fact that the primary annual maneuvers are naval training operations in the Arabian Sea.

The biggest and most effective of the treaty organizations is, of course, NATO, the North Atlantic Treaty Organization. It is composed, as its name implies, of fifteen nations located in the general vicinity of the North Atlantic Ocean: Belgium, Denmark, West Germany, Iceland, Luxembourg, Norway, Portugal, Turkey, the United States, Canada, France, Greece, Italy, the Netherlands, and the United Kingdom.

In the post-World War II era, the United States was forced to accept an unsought role of leadership in the free world. Ruined cities, demolished industries, bankrupt economies, and thousands of lives lost—these were the price paid for lack of unity among democratic nations of the world in 1939. After the 1918 Armistice in the "War to end war," democratic nations disarmed in the hopes that elimination of the tools of war would eliminate war. This approach to world peace failed miserably when the disciples of Hitler and Mussolini overran Europe. Efforts to end aggression by negotiation were to no avail.

World War II could not have been avoided without submission of free peoples to dictatorship. As a result, the most costly war of the ages was waged. When it was over, the Soviet Union was the only nation to reap substantial territorial gains. The program of encroachment and engulfment should have been a warning of Russia's grasping, imperialistic ambitions. After the war, the Soviets continued to expand control over eastern Europe by political infiltration and subversion. In the face of this westward thrust by the Communists, the nations of the free world finally decided to unite forces in order to cope with the immense Soviet military strength gathered in eastern Europe.

Between the end of World War II and the creation of the North Atlantic Treaty Organization on April 4, 1949, the Soviet Union extended its empire at a rate of 220,000 acres per day. Finland, Estonia, Latvia, Lithuania, Poland, Czechoslovakia, Romania, East Germany, Hungary, Bulgaria, Yugoslavia, and Albania all became satellite colonies of the Communist empire.

Since the defensive NATO alliance was created, there have been no further aggressions. Together, the NATO nations achieved what separately they could never have done alone; they stopped further aggression. Through unity and strength, they did what they had failed to do by concession and weakness in 1939.

But the accomplishments of NATO have been far greater than just halting aggression in Europe. This oceanic alliance has emphasized the cooperative progress of all its members, working in close partnership based upon common interests. Politically, member nations have recognized the increasing need for consultation about policies involving not only North Atlantic and European nations, but other troubled areas of the world as well. Economically and socially, NATO has provided a foundation upon which member nations can work toward development of new opportunities for all regions of the North Atlantic.

Militarily, NATO is faced with the need to cope with various forms of conventional, non-nuclear conflict and at the same time it must prevent escalation of strife of any type into nuclear war. NATO thus needs to maintain a strong role in the field of strategic nuclear deterrence as well as conventional power. Sea power's role in both areas is considerable. Conventional forces represented by the American Sixth Fleet in the Mediterranean and other Atlantic Fleet units in northern waters are in position to meet any challenge of land attack upon one or all NATO nations. Seaborne nuclear deterrents increase constantly in importance as nationalistic pressures pull at the very roots of NATO foundations. This is true because seaborne forces need not involve any territorial rights which can be and have been the cause of disagreement. Furthermore, it makes better political sense to deploy nuclear-tipped missiles at sea rather than locate them in heavily populated European regions. Twice during this century, Europe has suffered the devastation of total war. It is only natural that the presence of weapons which constitute primary targets in any nuclear exchange would create uneasiness among European peoples. Seaborne missiles are not targets which would endanger great masses of men, women, and children. Therefore, a logical extension of the Polaris missile concept would be to place this weapon in a naval fleet configured along merchant vessel lines because of simplicity of construction and operation. Such a move would relieve American missile responsibilities which now exist upon the continent of Europe.

One suggestion along these lines has been the possible creation of a multinational fleet, owned and controlled multilaterally by as many NATO nations as desired to participate. A unique feature of the proposal is that ships would be mixed-manned throughout by officers and men from participating nations. Experiments in mixed-manning of warships have been carried out successfully. This concept of seagoing, multinational nuclear missile forces first was advanced during the Presidential administration of General Dwight D. Eisenhower. It was hoped that such a force would curb dangerous proliferation of national nuclear arsenals. With such a multinational force, European nations could participate in nuclear deterrence without the expense or danger of building independent nuclear weapons. Furthermore, a truly integrated force could provide practical experience in working together for peoples of participating nations. Such an experience could lead to new cooperative ventures within the Atlantic partnership. Countries which join in owning, manning, and managing a major nuclear force are likely to find themselves drawn into increasingly intimate relations in many other ways.

With or without the refinements of a multilateral nuclear fleet, the burden of nuclear deterrence is bound to shift more and more to the Navy's seagoing forces and away from the ground units based on the continent of Europe. This added responsibility will further increase the demands made upon the United States Navy in meeting the many requirements of a policy of graduated deterrence, for the Navy already has a major role in responding to the many diverse challenges of a cold war which periodically flares into a limited hot war.

⚓

CHAPTER FIVE

The Cold War—An Exercise
in Graduated Deterrence

A cold shoulder and a cold winter during a scorching war set the stage for a cold war of long duration.

After Adolf Hitler scored his initial successes in the *Blitzkrieg* of 1939, he made overtures to the Soviet Union, seeking an alliance which would permit Germany to conquer western Europe and the British Isles while the Communists concentrated on the conquest of eastern Europe and all of Asia. Hitler believed a Russian-German alliance would be unbeatable. He may have been right. History will never know.

Soviet negotiator V. M. Molotov adamantly insisted that German troops get out of the Romanian Tyrol. Nazi Ambassador Joachim von Ribbentrop refused. Molotov stubbornly turned a cold shoulder to any further alliance conversations, whereupon Hitler's armies invaded Russia, forging a scorched earth path all the way to Stalingrad. But the vastness of Russia and the bitterness of its winters stopped the German advance in the same way they had halted Napoleon a century earlier. When the United States came to the aid of the Soviets with military supplies, the Communists bludgeoned the Germans back to their homeland, and in so doing, occupied much of eastern Europe.

Although the Soviets were always diffident partners in the western alliance, concentrating all their military energies upon Germany, Premier Joseph Stalin was included in Allied summit conferences at Yalta and Potsdam where the pattern of the postwar world was

47

set. It was agreed by everyone that the peoples of all occupied zones would be afforded the right of self-determination as one of the basic tenets of the freedoms for which the war was being fought. These occupied zones should have included Soviet-occupied Poland, East Germany, Austria, Hungary, the Balkans, and North Korea. But the Soviets reneged. Not once did the citizens of zones under Russian control have a voice in determining their own form of government. Instead, Communist satraps were installed to rule these nations, as they were brought behind the iron curtain when it was rung down. The world became divided into two camps—Communist and free.

Thus began the cold war.

The free world has lived up to its commitments to a policy of self-determination. Where aggression has been the tool of Communist expansion, force has been used to counter it. But force has not been used by the free world to extend its own influence over nations under Communist domination. The United States, independently and through the United Nations, adopted a policy of assisting any independent nation desiring to stem the tide of Communist aggression.

This is the essence of the cold war which has been raging since victory in Europe in 1945. The cold war forces upon the United States tremendous responsibilities. As leader of the free world, this nation must maintain forces in the proper number, in the proper proportions, and with the proper versatility to discourage aggression of any type or any level of intensity without escalating to nuclear war. And it must be willing to use these forces, as it has in Korea and Vietnam where the commitments have been heavy.

Nuclear deterrence has been a key component of United States strategy since the development of atomic weapons. Every event which has taken place on the international scene since 1945 has been under the shadow of the dreaded mushroom cloud. World leaders are fully aware of the tragic consequences of total nuclear war. Hiroshima and Nagasaki graphically demonstrated the destructive power of the atom bomb. Since then, nuclear weapons have increased a thousandfold in their potency. It is generally conceded that the death and destruction which would be suffered by both sides in a nuclear exchange would be unacceptable to either. But, as long as one side maintains a nuclear capability, the other must maintain a similar force. Failure to do this might be nothing short of suicide. Such is the slender thread of nuclear stalemate upon which the very survival of humanity hangs.

The Cuban incident was a nearly successful attempt to unbalance the tenuous scales of nuclear power by placing missiles close to United States shores. When the attempt was detected before the missiles were ready for firing, President John F. Kennedy responded with an immediate naval quarantine to stop further entry of missiles into Cuba and to force withdrawal of those delivered. The ships of the Second Fleet built a fence around Cuba with the determination, if necessary, to shoot non-nuclear weapons to block future expansion of Communist atomic missile capabilities. But standing there silently, unseen behind the conventional forces, was the tremendous nuclear power of the Polaris fleet ballistic missile submarines. In the face of the stark realities of nuclear war, the Soviets backed down. This was deterrence in its rawest, most dangerous, but also its most effective state. The Polaris fleet shoulders the Navy's primary responsibilities in the strategy of nuclear deterrence. Polaris is this nation's silent answer to blustering Communist nuclear sword-rattling.

But there are lesser wars and conflicts which must be deterred or extinguished if they burst into flame. In 1960, the United States came to the realization that it could not halt or even check "brush-fire" wars, could not stop infiltration, could not combat insurgency within new nations merely by brandishing the threat of retaliation by strategic nuclear forces. From this realization came a concept of graduated deterrence. In other words, which are those of Gilbert and Sullivan, "Let the punishment fit the crime." Let the military and political responses to any crisis fit the needs of that particular situation.

Graduated deterrence means applying the proper forces at the proper time to meet whatever aggressive challenge may arise, whether it be an attack upon warships sailing the high seas, or the strangling of a free-world friend in a Vietnamese rice paddy. Where this practice had been put into effect without formal recognition of such a concept, the results were spectacular. When Red activity created a war in Greece, the national government turned to the United States. Under General James A. Van Fleet, army and navy advisers and equipment turned the tide. The Greeks resisted and with United States help remained free. Yugoslavia, Bulgaria, Albania did not.

While still preoccupied with massive nuclear deterrence, the United States was drawn into still another war in Korea. Divided at the 38th parallel by the Potsdam Agreement of August, 1945, South Korea was looked upon hungrily by the Communists when the United States forces withdrew in 1948. The Communists moved to swallow up all of that peninsular nation in June, 1950. United Nations forces, under American leadership, responded to throw back the enemy while containing the war within the Korean Peninsula. Had the conflict spread to Manchuria and China, there might have been no limit to where the flames of war could have reached.

These were shooting wars, as is the war in Vietnam, where aggression is again being countered. Naval forces are taking important parts in the fighting. Carrier-borne naval aircraft are proving most effective for controlled, deliberate response. Sea-based Marines have been called upon for emergency augmentation of land forces. American patrol craft have been used to curb arms traffic from the North.

Forces of deterrence must also be able to prevent shooting. This might be accomplished by the mere presence of an amphibious force able and ready to meet any eventuality. The Lebanon landing was a dramatic example of this level of graduated deterrence. Threatened with a revolt that could have ended only with the loss of this free-world friend to communism, the Lebanese officials called for help. Within a matter of hours after this plea was voiced, U.S. Sixth Fleet Marines were ashore. The situation was stabilized and a free nation was saved without firing a shot.

Varying degrees of deterrent pressure have been exerted before and since then by this nation to extinguish dangerous flames in such world hot spots as Suez, Jordan, Quemoy-Matsu, the Dominican Republic, the Congo, Berlin, Guatemala, and Thailand. At the lowest end of the spectrum of graduated deterrence are the "goodwill" visits of United States naval units—displaying the flag, serving to improve understanding among peoples, making friends throughout the world. This offers a prescription in preventive medicine. In military operations, as well as elsewhere, "An ounce of prevention is worth a pound of cure." Although far from being dramatic, the everyday visits by Navy and Marine Corps ambassadors of goodwill have created a favorable image of the American people among peoples of Africa, Europe, Asia, South America, and all the rest of the world. This is a vital weapon for peace.

The unique capabilities of the United States Navy, operating without reliance upon treaties or expensive bases, to perform a vital mission of graduated deterrence are brought out in a story circulated through Washington, D.C., during one Middle Eastern crisis.

As the situation went from bad to worse—so the story goes—the Chiefs of Staff were called together at the Pentagon to decide upon a course of action.

"What can you do?" the Army Chief of Staff was asked.

"Give me the ships and airplanes and I can move a division of troops there," was the reply.

"What can you do?" the Air Force Chief of Staff was queried.

"Tell me which city you want blown off the face of the earth and I will do it," came the reply.

When the same question was posed to the Chief of Naval Operations, the answer was "Nothing."

After the shock had its effect, the admiral added, "I ordered the Sixth Fleet there last night."

The anecdote may be fiction, but it does illustrate the ability to use naval forces for implementing a policy of graduated deterrence.

As a crisis brews, self-contained naval units are on the move carrying a wide range of aircraft, from fighters to bombers, plus substantial numbers of Marine and Seabee amphibious forces to the scene. These forces have the capability for shore bombardment, reconnaissance, amphibious landings—in short, any military requirement that they may be asked to meet. They are ready for immediate action. They can go into action, or merely steam close to shore to

51

display clearly the might of the United States. Or, they can stay over the horizon so that they can sail quietly away with no one aware that they were there, should their presence not be required.

The Navy is ready for any contingency in carrying out international relations, as it has been since the early years of our independence. However, in this critical period the missions of the Navy in the field of foreign affairs continue to grow, for it is the epitome of a versatile, mobile strategy of graduated deterrence which is a national policy required to meet the challenges of communism. Since its inception, communist ideology has maintained an avowed and oft-stated purpose of world domination. Its timetable is not fixed. The Communists are willing to wait one hundred years or more to achieve this ultimate goal, but in the interim every opportunity will be exploited in order to undermine governments of free nations and, through infiltration, to divide and conquer.

We must be able and willing to respond for the preservation of freedom.

⚓

CHAPTER SIX

The Evolution of
American Naval Power

Since the dawn of history, the cheapest way to go anywhere has been on the water in a boat. As ships began to move across the seas for economic, political, and social purposes, it followed logically that military forces were developed to protect them and to disrupt similar excursions by competitors. Soon nations established areas of influence over the seas and the evolution of sea power was under way.

The Egyptians were the first known people to build ships of any size, but it was the Greeks who developed the world's first truly effective fighting ships—the galleys rowed by one or two hundred men seated in one, two, or three banks. Greek oarsmen could spin a huge, 200-foot-long, shallow draft warship on its axis or they could drive it forward or backward with equal facility. Entire fleets maneuvered with the precision of a well-trained drill team. The Greek galley's primary weapon was the sturdy ram which protruded from the bow at the water's edge. With flashing oars, the galleys first crippled their enemies by slashing through the oars of their opponents, and then with the concerted force of hundreds of men at the long sweeps, they plunged headlong into the broadsides of their foe. Few wooden ships could withstand the impact of the solid battering ram.

The galley was the principal Mediterranean man-of-war for more than 2,000 years. The ram, invented by the Greeks 2,800 years ago, still was proving its worth as late as the American Civil War. It was with these weapons that the first naval battle of historical significance was fought in 480 B.C. Attacking Persians had overrun parts of Greece, even capturing Athens. A final push to total victory was to be made by thousands of warriors, the cream of the Persian army, carried in a massive fleet of 1,200 ships. Standing in their way was the Greek navy at Salamis. Although only 400 in number, the Greek ships were manned by well-trained, disciplined, experienced, and knowledgeable seamen. Taking full advantage of their superior nautical skills and understanding of currents, winds, and waves, the defenders trapped the invaders in a narrow strait. With unrelenting wind and tide against their backs and the hard-pressing Greek fleet in their faces, the Persian navy was destroyed with the loss of more than 20,000 lives. So complete and decisive was their defeat that the invaders limped back to Asia, leaving Greece free to extend its own influence throughout the eastern Mediterranean. Greece prospered and became the foundation of a great western civilization.

At the western end of the Mediterranean, the influence of sea power was not decisive until nearly three centuries later when Rome was challenged by Carthage. The Romans denied Carthage the use of the seas around the Italian peninsula. This forced Hannibal to march overland from Spain, through France, and across the Alps in order to invade Italy. This magnificent but tremendously costly excursion was successful initially. However, Roman sea power prevented reinforcements and supplies from reaching Hannibal. Rome ultimately eroded the strength of the foreign intruders and ejected them.

Two centuries before Christ was born, Rome learned well the lessons of sea power and began to amass sizable military and merchant fleets. Caesar used the seas to spread his influence northward through Europe and into the British Isles. Octavian, by routing the fleet of Mark Antony and Cleopatra at Actium in 31 B.C., completed consolidation of the Roman Empire. Wide use of military and merchant shipping spread Octavian's influence and Roman culture throughout the civilized world of that day, converting the entire Mediterranean Sea into a private lake.

During the Dark Ages, only the hardy, ferocious Norsemen ranged far to sea. Vikings sailed west to the hemisphere of the Americas and south to England and France. In the ninth century, they even found their way into the Mediterranean. Unlike southern Europeans who turned seaward in the later years of the Renaissance, these fierce Scandinavians concentrated upon fighting, pillaging, and plunder. The Vikings failed to exploit the economic advantages of their discoveries.

Columbus' discovery of America on an economic quest for shorter routes to India opened a new era for Spain and Portugal who capitalized fully upon the riches of these new lands. This forced Spain to don, not unwillingly, the mantle of the world's leading sea power. She wore this cloak well for a century, despite the growing naval power of England, Holland, and France, and in the Mediterranean where Muhammadanism experienced a phenomenal rise to power both on land and sea. Under the skillful guidance of able Sultan Suleiman, the Magnificent, the Turks pressed their armies up the Balkan peninsula to the gates of Vienna. But victory at Lepanto in 1571, by the fleet under Don Juan of Austria, was heralded throughout Christendom as finally stopping the spread of Islamism throughout the world. The battle took place off the shores of Greece, only a short distance from Salamis. Except for the addition of a few crude guns, ships and tactics were the same as those of two thousand years earlier when the Greeks repulsed the invading Persians. However, this was the end of an era. Lepanto was the last major sea engagement to be fought between ships propelled by oars.

Naval warfare was undergoing the first of many dramatic changes to be witnessed in the centuries to follow—changes which continue to be made today at a rapid pace. Early in the sixteenth century, King Henry VIII set this transition in motion by modernizing the British fleet and introducing the revolutionary broadside battery of heavy guns. Queen Elizabeth continued the expansion of the navy which trained by raiding the outposts of the vast maritime empire of Spain.

In 1588, Philip of Spain sent forth an "invincible" armada to invade England. The challenge was met by Sir Francis Drake. With revolutionary tactics, Drake's ships stood off and fought with gunfire, rather than closing and boarding the enemy for hand-to-hand combat. The Spanish, unprepared to fight in this manner, took a heavy pounding during a ten-day running battle and then fled northward around the British Isles. Violent North Atlantic storms completed the devastation started by Drake's guns. More than half of the tall Spanish galleons which had sailed so proudly from Lisbon never returned. The back of the Spanish military might was broken so completely that Spain could not defend herself as other nations gobbled up her empire.

Subsequently, England, France, and Holland all satisfied their territorial appetites at the expense of Spain. These three middle-European nations vied for domination of the seven seas, but Holland was eliminated by the British by 1714 in a battle off the mouth of the Thames River. Since England and France, the remaining competitors, held large colonial interests in the new world, the Western Hemisphere became the scene of greatly increased naval activity. At the outset of the American War of Independence, the colonists had no navy and would have been at the mercy of the British fleet if the French navy had not served as a deterrent and distraction which forced England to spread its fleet thinly throughout the world. Thus British sea power could not concentrate upon quelling the American Revolution.

In one way or another, the ingenious, independence-minded colonists soon acquired a nucleus of ships-of-the-line. The first sea action of the Revolution took place in June, 1775, when Jeremiah O'Brien mobilized citizens of Machias, Maine, to capture a British sloop loaded with lumber. After a heated battle with muskets, axes, and pitchforks, the British midshipman commander was killed and the colonists had captured their first ship. O'Brien hoisted the Pine Tree flag and embarked upon a career of raiding British commerce along the Maine coast.

This was the inception of the Colonial Navy.

In 1775, the Continental Congress authorized the purchase and fitting out of eight small ships which were placed under the command of Esek Hopkins. John Paul Jones, the most renowned Revolutionary naval hero, began his eminent career in this force. In one of his early commands, the *Ranger*, Jones proposed that a French man-of-war salute the American flag. This was the first recognition of the independence of American colonies by France. The dashing Jones took the war to England's own shores, raiding beaches and coastal towns. The capture of the British sloop *Drake* off the coast of England and the subsequent exchange of prisoners, the first such trade of the war, inspired the admiration of the King of France. The American captain and his close friend, Ben Franklin, persuaded France to give more aid to the colonists and also to fit out an old merchant hull as an American fighting ship.

Jones renamed his new ship *Bon Homme Richard* in honor of Franklin's *Poor Richard's Almanac* and sailed in company with a French force under Pierre Landais. Challenged by the British ship *Serapis,* Jones was urged to surrender the battered *Richard.*

"I have not yet begun to fight," was the American's immortal reply. Victory belonged to Jones that day. He captured the *Serapis* without the assistance of the rascally Landais who actually fired on the American. *Bon Homme Richard* was sinking when the battle ended, so Jones transferred to *Serapis* and sailed to Holland.

American independence finally came when Admiral de Grasse's French fleet blocked the sea approaches to the Chesapeake Bay, denying reinforcements to Lord Cornwallis while George Washington attacked British land forces with impunity. Cornwallis' surrender ended British efforts to put down the Revolution.

And thus, this nation was born.

After the Revolution, the American Navy was allowed to wither away, as has happened after every war. It soon became apparent, however, that the United States, as rich as it was in natural resources, could not live alone and be self-sufficient. This led to a great expansion of overseas trade. The need for a navy to protect this merchant shipping was instantly felt. The United States Navy was established with the traditions, organization, and regulations of the British which it was soon to battle.

Old Ironsides, as the USS *Constitution* became known when cannonballs bounced off her oaken sides, and the other ships, USS *Constellation* and USS *United States*, put to sea in 1798 as the foundation of the U.S. Navy. The fledgling navy "cut its eyeteeth" in the decade to follow in an undeclared war with France and by battling Barbary pirates who preyed upon American merchant shipping in the Mediterranean.

While the American Navy was making its initial mark upon the world of sea power, the British navy, brought to a high peak of efficiency by the immortal Horatio Nelson, achieved the height of its glory at sea. Napoleon had scored significant successes in Europe and hungered to attack the British homeland. Nelson shattered Bonaparte's invasion dreams at Trafalgar in 1805, when opposing fleets crashed head on in the last great battle of massed sailing ships.

The combined French and Spanish fleet possessed superiority in numbers, but it was no match for the daring and tactical wizardry of the one-armed, one-eyed Admiral Nelson, whose fleet stormed through the center of the French-Spanish battle line. In the melee that followed, Nelson's ships chewed up major sections of the enemy fleet. Nelson, cut down by a sniper as the ships continued the battle at close range, was one of the greatest naval tacticians the world has ever known. Under his leadership and inspiration, Nelson's navy not only defended the British Isles from invasion by France and Spain, but later, by controlling the seas, set the stage for the defeat of Napoleon at Waterloo. At Trafalgar, Nelson's battle order was, "England expects every man to do his duty." As Nelson died later the same day, his last words were, "Thank God, I have done my duty."

The British "ruled the waves" for more than four centuries, but domination of the oceans of the world demanded the maintenance of a sizable fleet. When personnel problems became acute, the British resorted to the simple recruiting technique of kidnapping sailors from American merchant ships. The War of 1812 resulted. The fledgling U.S. Navy proved it could win ship-to-ship duels with units of the mighty British fleet. The spirit displayed by Captain James Lawrence as he lay dying on the decks of the USS *Chesapeake* carried the new navy through many tight scrapes, making up for what it lacked in experience and firepower. His order, "Don't give up the ship," still lives today.

During the War of 1812, many major actions occurred in Atlantic waters, but one of the decisive naval engagements was on the inland waters of Lake Champlain. In the fall of 1814, an American squadron under the command of Commodore Thomas Macdonough repulsed a Canadian invasion force which sought to use the lake route to the Hudson River and thus to New York. Control of the Great Lakes by American sea power again prevented large-scale movement of invasion troops from the north. When British commanders realized that the American domination of the colonies could not be broken, they advised London to seek peace. The Treaty of Ghent was signed on Christmas eve, 1814.

The United States Navy proved its ability to control limited areas, such as the Great Lakes, and individual ships proved to be a match for single units of the British fleet, but the American fleet in no way threatened to dislodge Britain as the leading nineteenth-century sea power of an oceanic world. It did, however, earn a reputation as a maritime power to be reckoned with. The reputation was broadened as the U.S. Navy improved tactics and gained valuable experience fighting pirates of the Mediterranean and Caribbean and the Malays of the Far East. The U.S. Navy, soon to enter the age of steam and steel, grew up in the days of sail, wooden ships, and iron men.

The American Civil War marked a historic era of transition and innovation in tactics and weapons of naval warfare and hastened greatly the maturing process of the United States Navy.

The relatively inconclusive battle of the ironclads *Monitor* and *Merrimac* was the most significant naval action of the war. This was the first practical demonstration of the value of armor in ships. As a result, the U.S. Navy led the world in the construction of steel ships in the years to follow. Innovation, however, was prevalent in all elements of naval warfare during the Civil War. The screw propeller provided far greater efficiency with less vulnerability when compared to old side- or stern-wheelers. John Dahlgren developed the smooth-bore cannon to the greatest possible degree. Smoothbores had their limitations, however. They were most accurate when the cannonball skipped or ricocheted across the water into the side of the enemy ship. This could be effective only at ranges of up to one mile. Rifled guns, first developed for the army, soon were adapted to naval use by Robert Parrott. Accuracy and range increased tremendously. Ships no longer depended for victory upon how the cannonball bounced.

Another Civil War innovation was the primitive torpedo, which was more like a mine than today's underwater missile. The Confederates led the development of this effective weapon. They also launched the world's first torpedo boat, a small craft with an explosive charge lashed to a boom protruding from the front of the craft. But it proved as hazardous to the attacker as to the defender.

New ideas were not limited to weapons. It was in the Civil War and the Mexican conflict that the Navy first knew steam under battle conditions. It had much to learn about the new propulsion system, but it learned quickly and oftentimes ingeniously. Lieutenant Edward Baker tells of chasing a fast Confederate blockade runner with the U.S. steamer *Pocahontas* which he commanded. The Confederate was a match for the Union steamer, but Lieutenant Baker, not hindered by safety regulations, fed generous quantities of bacon and ham into the boiler fireboxes to get the "superheat" needed to gain the extra steam to produce the added speed for victory.

For twenty years after the Civil War, the American Navy was grossly neglected. President Chester A. Arthur, recognizing the need for this nation to expand its horizons, commenced rebuilding the fleets, a task which was completed by President Theodore Roosevelt, who is credited with being the "father" of the modern American Navy.

Roosevelt's influence upon the United States Navy was felt long before he became President. As Assistant Secretary of the Navy, the later-famed Rough Rider insisted upon excellence of fleet gunnery and operations. It was he who initiated gunnery practice by naval vessels. Roosevelt also set the stage for George Dewey's brilliant victory in the Philippines, by arranging to have the dashing commodore named commander of the Western Pacific Squadron. Well before hostilities broke out, Roosevelt ordered Dewey to capture Manila when fighting commenced.

This investment in overall excellence of the fleet paid huge dividends in the Spanish-American War. In the brief few months of active fighting, the U.S. Fleet repeatedly scored spectacular successes against the Spanish, whose fleet had previously been considered superior.

The Spanish-American War is characterized by pictures of Theodore Roosevelt storming up San Juan Hill, but this was truly a naval war from start to finish. The sinking of the USS *Maine*, sent to Havana to protect American citizens, aroused public opinion in the United States. As a result, ten days after Congress declared war on April 21, 1898, Commodore Dewey slipped into Manila Bay before dawn to surprise and destroy the Spanish Philippine fleet at anchor without damage to his own forces. The victory gave the United States a vital American naval base which it continues to use today.

In the Atlantic, Admiral William T. Sampson successfully bottled up the Spanish fleet in Santiago, with final victory coming on July 3, when Admiral Cervera attempted to break out of the Yankee blockade. The entire Spanish fleet was destroyed with all its people killed or captured. One American was killed.

The pattern of political growth of much of the Caribbean was established that day. Cervera's defeat, coming so close on the heels of Dewey's victory in Manila, led to a peace treaty by which Spain withdrew from the region discovered by Columbus. In addition to the Pacific bases in the Philippines and Guam, the United States acquired a naval base in Cuba, whose independence it guaranteed, and also Puerto Rico.

The latter part of the nineteenth century was also marked by a greater realization of the importance of strategy and tactics. This was reflected in the establishment of the Naval War College at Newport, Rhode Island, where naval officers could undertake postgraduate schooling in military, political, and economic fields.

As the United States entered the twentieth century, Theodore Roosevelt adopted a foreign policy of "speak softly and carry a big stick." The United States Navy was Roosevelt's "big stick." President Roosevelt expanded the Navy, and under his leadership the battleship emerged as the backbone of the modern Navy. Roosevelt set out to show the world that in the American Navy the British who boasted that the sun never set on its navy had a rival for the first time in more than a century. To put this new Navy on display, Roosevelt painted the battleship fleet white and ordered it to sail around the world. The Great White Fleet of sixteen glistening battleships cruised 46,000 miles, leaving Hampton Roads, Virginia, in 1908 to sail around Cape Horn to San Francisco and then across the Pacific to Japan via the Hawaiian Islands. Australia, South Asia, and the Suez Canal were visited. In the Mediterranean, the fleet rendered timely assistance to southern Italy and Sicily, hit by a disastrous earthquake, before returning across the Atlantic to its home base in Virginia.

Not only did the cruise reap strong benefits in international goodwill, but experience gained had lasting technical rewards for the U.S. Navy. Engineers proved the ability of ships to be sustained for long periods at sea. Great strides were made in the improvement of gunnery. Experience in supplying a fleet overseas was invaluable. Politically and militarily the Navy became the nation's first line of defense, which it remains today.

As World War I approached, the nation continued to expand and improve its Navy, not only structurally but also in gunnery and fleet efficiency which had become the hallmarks of naval training. More and more emphasis was given to the training of the individual as well, so that naval service soon provided officers and enlisted men with valuable education. Personnel were encouraged to develop new ideas which were put into effect to bring the fleet to peak efficiency. This was an educational revolution for naval personnel.

In World War I, the principal mission of the United States Navy was that of escorting troops and supplies across the Atlantic to beleaguered allies in Europe. Antisubmarine countermeasures were developed quickly under the able guidance of Admiral William S. Sims whose destroyers escorted a steady flow of ships across the Atlantic in spite of heavy losses. The United States entered the war too late for the Navy to participate in the most significant surface action of the war, the Battle of Jutland. More than 260 ships—150 British and 111 German—were massed for this battle. The entire fleets never actually joined in combat, for the Germans tried to isolate portions of the British fleet to bring local superiority to bear. Several duels, costly to both sides, resulted. At the crucial point, the British, under Admiral Sir John Jellicoe, achieved a strategic position from which they should have destroyed the remaining fleet, but the Germans, under the command of Admiral Reinhard Scheer, escaped by previously untried precision maneuvering under the cover of smoke. The German fleet never again ventured forth. From that day forward, the Germans concentrated on submarine warfare, which ultimately brought the United States into the conflict on the side of the British.

Jutland was the beginning of the end of the battleship fleets, although it was not until a quarter of a century later that most of the peoples of the world recognized this. Watching over Jutland was the battleship's successor, the airplane. The British ship *Engadine*, the world's first aircraft carrier, had launched a seaplane to contact and report the disposition of the German fleet. This was the first use of the airplane at sea in a naval battle.

During the interim between world wars, the U.S. Navy was entangled in an internal struggle. The "gun club" admirals, traditionalists who relied on the battleship and naval gunfire, discounted the importance of aircraft. A new breed of naval officer, the aviators, opposed them, looking to the sky instead.

Pearl Harbor settled the argument with eight battleships resting on the bottom. As such the battleship fleet seemed dead. Although the "dreadnoughts" did prove their worth later in the war, they were no longer the principal capital ship of the United States Navy.

The aircraft carrier became the reigning queen of the seas, a position which she still holds today. The aircraft carrier was not the only star of the show in the war of the forties, for World War II was a war of balanced forces. The full resources of the entire Navy and all other branches of the armed forces of this nation were required for victory.

The infantry, carried into battle by the Navy, was needed to slug out final victory in Europe as well as across the islands of the Pacific to Okinawa. The Air Force, supplied with fuel and ammunition by naval convoys, was needed for air support to the Army. The Navy sought out and sank enemy merchant and naval fleets to starve out the industrial and military capacity of the foe and to ensure free movement of supplies and troops of our allies and our own forces overseas. Behind all this was the need for full utilization of the industrial complex and the civilian support required to operate it.

It was truly a total war.

The Navy fought in every element available to it, on the seas, over the seas, and under the seas. And the Navy fought on land as well as on sea—through its unique ability to bombard beaches on a round-the-clock schedule; through its air arm which carried the war hundreds of miles inland; and through its Marine assault troops.

Submarines battled all types of ships, including other submarines. Aircraft fought other planes, surface ships, submarines, and land targets. Ship-to-ship engagements, thought to be outmoded by many early in 1942, cost this nation a half-dozen cruisers, more than a dozen destroyers, and several other types of ships before the end of the first year of war. By 1945, even aircraft carriers were to find themselves involved in surface actions, and surface ships were finding themselves attacking railroad trains as a diversion from their normal responsibilities of engaging enemy ships, convoying our own troops and supplies.

And the battleships, which suffered so tragically at Pearl Harbor, later proved their worth both as escorts to carriers and for bombardment support to amphibious operations.

The basic problem of the Navy in the Atlantic was ferrying troops, supporting amphibious landings where troops went ashore against enemy opposition. The first United States offensive in the Atlantic was Operation Torch, the landing of U.S. troops at Casablanca in North Africa. Admiral H. Kent Hewitt successfully crossed the Atlantic with more than 150 troopships. The greatest of all amphibious operations, however, was General Dwight Eisenhower's Operation Overlord, the landing on the Normandy coast. The Navy cleared enemy gun emplacements and ensured success by defending the landing troops against air attacks. With a fleet of 4,000 ships, the Allied navies kept a steady flow of equipment and ammunition moving to ground forces as they fought into Germany for victory.

The Pacific War was the Navy's war from the crushing day of infamy, Pearl Harbor, December 7, 1941, to August 27, 1945, when the Third Fleet under the command of Admiral William F. Halsey sailed victoriously into Tokyo Bay.

In the Pacific War, for the first time in history, naval air power was the dominating factor. Without the control of the skies, provided by American carrier planes, the advance of amphibious forces across the Pacific against well-established land-based air fleets would have been impossible. The guiding hand for this massive naval war in which the airplane played such a great part was a destroyer and submarine sailor, Fleet Admiral Chester W. Nimitz, who proved as commander in chief of the Pacific Fleet to be one of the world's most able military strategists and an outstanding administrator. While the nation still reeled under the shock of Pearl Harbor, and the assault continued upon the Philippines and other outposts in the Pacific, the Navy struck back. Under Halsey's command, a U.S. carrier task force hit the Marshall and Gilbert Islands. Less than six months after the Japanese attack, the Navy carried Army Air Corps bombers to within less than seven hundred miles of Japanese shores. Lieutenant Colonel James Doolittle's raid on Tokyo on April 18, 1942, was launched from the Navy aircraft carrier USS *Hornet*. War was brought to the Japanese homeland but it was to take another three years of bitter fighting before the American fleet could return to Japanese waters in strength.

Seizure of Guadalcanal on August 7, 1942, in the first American amphibious operation of the Pacific War touched off a series of ship-to-ship night actions which claimed a heavy toll of American forces. Over a period of four months these surface actions claimed the United States cruisers *Astoria, Quincy, Vincennes, Atlanta, Juneau,* and *Northampton,* and the Australian cruiser *Canberra.* The battleship *South Dakota* and cruisers *San Francisco, Chicago, Boise, Portland, Helena, Pensacola, New Orleans,* and *Minneapolis* were damaged heavily by surface fire. Eleven destroyers were sunk and eight others damaged.

As American cruisers engaged Japanese battleships, the toll almost wiped out the entire United States cruiser forces in the Pacific, but the defense of the Marine and Army troops ashore in Guadalcanal was successful. The ground forces were there to stay. The Tokyo Express which threatened to isolate Australia and New Zealand from the United States had been stopped. The tide of the war had changed. The United States forces were on their way to Japan, although the road across the vast Pacific was long and tortuous. Guadalcanal, Tarawa, Guam, the Philippines, Iwo Jima, and Okinawa were the bloody way stations as the United States' island-hopping campaign forged westward toward Japan.

For the most part, fleet engagements were aerial battles. Japan, for instance, brought to Midway eleven battleships, including the mighty *Yamato*, mounting the world's largest naval guns—nine 18-inch cannons. This armada never came within one hundred miles of a surface target.

Only in the Battle of Leyte Gulf were the older American battleships pitted against Japanese counterparts in a traditional surface engagement. As the American Army forces under General Douglas MacArthur made their landings on Leyte in the Philippines, the Japanese made a determined naval attempt to drive them off. By dividing their attack into three prongs, the Japanese violated a naval warfare principle of concentration of effort, but they almost succeeded.

A southern force of the Japanese fleet approached the Leyte landings through Surigao Strait. There they were met and virtually destroyed by old United States battleships, cruisers, destroyers, and motor torpedo boats under the command of Rear Admiral J. B. Oldendorf whose force had been primarily prepared for shore bombardment. He actually succeeded "in crossing the T." The northern Japanese force, primarily a decoy and consisting mainly of aircraft carriers without airplanes, succeeded in enticing Admiral Halsey to chase it northward with his modern battleships and heavy aircraft carriers. This left the gate open at San Bernardino Straits through which passed the Japanese central force led by the 85,000-ton *Yamato* and including four battleships and five cruisers. Although Admiral Kurita did not realize it, the way was now open for him to enter Leyte Gulf where he could have wrought havoc with General Douglas MacArthur's transports which were in the process of unloading. Only six escort carriers stood between Admiral Kurita and the landing operations in Leyte Gulf. The strangest surface action of all times, battleships against aircraft carriers, proved symbolic of the trend of naval warfare. Here, in the last fling of the battleship, the mighty "dreadnought," which once ruled the waves, had a chance for revenge upon the type of ship which succeeded it as queen of the seas. But the Japanese battleship commander failed to realize his opportunity. With his guns he sank two American jeep carriers and damaged the others heavily, but then retired without finishing the job and without molesting the landing operations which he had come to destroy.

The battleship has sailed into oblivion. Its only hope for revival is in its unique shore-bombardment capabilities. Except for that, the battleship is outmoded. All the battleships in the world have been retired. None are being built to replace them.

The climax of the Pacific War was the invasion of Okinawa. An armada of 1,300 ships launched and supported the landings which took place April 1, 1945, Easter Sunday. After eighty-three days of fighting, the island was secured. The cost to the U.S. Navy was high—36 ships sunk, 369 damaged, and 763 aircraft lost. But the enemy's losses were even greater. More than 110,000 men were lost. The Japanese air force was virtually destroyed, with more than 7,800 aircraft destroyed, approximately 7,700 of them shot down in aerial combat.

While surface and air forces were clashing head on with the enemy, the American submarine fleet was performing a major role of strangling the Japanese war-making capacity. Submarines virtually destroyed the Japanese merchant marine and thereby prevented essential raw materials from reaching the island empire from the colonies it had annexed during the expansion of its Greater East Asia Co-Prosperity Sphere.

By the end of the war the United States Navy had assembled the greatest worldwide fleet the world had ever known—67,952 ships with 3,380,817 men and women wearing Navy blue. Eighty-seven per cent of these were reservists, most of whom were recruited, trained, and sent to sea for the first time after December 7.

Immediately after V-J Day, as has been the custom throughout American history, a speedy reduction of forces followed. Stripped of its fighting ability within days after the surrender ceremony, September 2, 1945, aboard the USS *Missouri*, the Navy shrank to only 671 ships, less than 1 per cent of what wartime Secretary of the Navy James Forrestal, later to become the first U.S. Secretary of Defense, described as the "greatest aggregation of sea and air power which the world has ever seen."

Korea necessitated a rebuilding of the Navy, with much the same operational responsibilities and format as in World War II. The Russian-directed-and-equipped North Koreans invaded the Republic of Korea. Defenders were driven almost into the sea. American Marine forces and Navy-transported Army units snatched the South Koreans from defeat when a 50-mile perimeter around Pusan was the only toehold the free world had in Korea. United Nations forces, supplied by naval units, forced their way back northward. A major advance was achieved through the amphibious operations at Inchon, brilliantly executed under the leadership of General Douglas MacArthur. Naval task forces moved up and down the coasts of Korea virtually unmolested as they attacked enemy targets all the way north to the Yalu River.

After Korea, the Navy did not suffer its usual postwar reduction but, instead, was stabilized in numbers to meet the many diverse responsibilities of a cold-war era. The four-ocean challenge which faces the United States Navy today imposes upon it more and greater missions than ever before in history, for the Navy must be prepared to meet every kind of challenge throughout the spectrum of war.

⚓

CHAPTER SEVEN

The Long Arm of Naval Air

The most versatile and effective weapon in today's modern navy is the task force built around the aircraft carrier. Wherever there has been trouble in the world, United States carrier forces have played an important role as mobile air bases complete with their own defenses.

The aircraft carrier striking force can go anywhere on the seven seas. Its aircraft can extend the long reach of sea power to virtually all corners of the world to apply immediate pressures on any trouble spot.

The success of the aircraft carrier striking force lies in its self-sufficiency and mobility, and in its unique power punch which can be applied wherever and whenever needed without relying on others for assistance. It offers an extra measure of international independence, for no other allied nation need be involved in any carrier operation nor share the responsibility for any actions, as must foreign hosts to American land-based aircraft.

Due to modern improved logistic supply methods, the carrier task force can remain indefinitely on station overseas. This "staying power" will be even further increased when all units are nuclear powered. The flexibility and mobility of a nuclear-powered carrier task force was demonstrated by the circumnavigation of the world without replenishing fuel or any other supplies by a task force composed of the carrier *Enterprise*, cruiser *Long Beach*, and guided missile frigate *Bainbridge*. New developments in nuclear propulsion plants hold promise of reactor cores which will last the lifetime of the ship itself. Thus the ship of tomorrow may never have to be refueled.

A half-century ago, stunt pilot Eugene Ely landed an airplane on the deck of the battleship *Pennsylvania* anchored in San Francisco Bay. Thus began the development of naval aviation which has since reached a degree unequaled by any other power.

The vastness of the Pacific Ocean first led the Navy to become interested in the construction of aircraft carriers. Admiral William A. Moffett, one of the Navy's first flying flag officers, envisioned the need for air power in any major world struggle. Special concern was felt about Japanese control of Pacific islands, which they had acquired as a result of World War I.

The Navy's first aircraft carrier was the converted coal ship USS *Langley,* a modest success. Admiral Moffett subsequently led a successful campaign for congressional authority to convert two battle-cruiser hulls under construction to aircraft carriers. These were the USS *Lexington* and USS *Saratoga.* Doubting, nonflying admirals insisted that these aircraft carriers retain their principal surface weapons, the 8-inch rifles of a heavy cruiser. Today the design of aircraft carriers has gone to the other extreme. The newest ships carry few or no guns even for defense purposes. The aircraft carrier depends entirely upon its planes and the guns and missiles of screening ships to protect it against surface or air attack. It relies upon its own long-range underwater sound-detection and ranging equipment—sonar—speed, maneuverability, and the weapons of screening destroyers, to defend it against submarine attacks.

The *Lexington* and the *Saratoga* were uneconomical to operate, but served as training bases for the rapid expansion of naval aviation. Soon they were joined by the USS *Ranger,* and later by the USS *Yorktown* and USS *Enterprise,* the first ships to be built as aircraft carriers from the keel up.

Before World War II, however, the importance of the aircraft carrier was not fully appreciated even within the United States Navy. Naval aviation proved its ability to extend the impact of sea power great distances in many fleet maneuvers dating back to the early thirties. Some traditionalists, however, continued to rate the battleship as the capital ship, or backbone of the Navy. They were aided unwittingly by the colorful General Billy Mitchell who personally

70

discounted the value of all navies and all armies. His successful bombing and sinking of a motionless target, the old battleship *Alabama,* and outmoded German warships, caused proponents of land-based air forces to unleash propaganda contending that their way of waging war would make infantry and naval forces obsolete. In the depression years, this found some appeal in the name of economy.

However, with the enlightened assistance of President Franklin D. Roosevelt, who served as Assistant Secretary of the Navy during World War I, and Representative Carl Vinson, chairman of the House Naval Affairs Committee, the Navy withstood the onslaught. These two stalwart advocates of sea power insisted upon building a larger navy and demanded more efficiency in maneuvers and tactics.

The Japanese were even quicker to realize the value of the aircraft carrier as a weapons system, and they built them at a rapid rate after they threw off the yoke of naval armament limitations. The Nipponese watched as carefully as the United States observers when the *Saratoga* and *Lexington* launched highly successful attacks upon Pearl Harbor as part of the 1932 and 1933 Pacific Fleet war games. The Japanese learned the lessons better than the Americans did. A year later, Commander Logan C. Ramsey forecast in a Naval Institute *Proceedings* article that the techniques used by the two United States aircraft carriers would someday be employed by the Japanese to strike Pearl Harbor. Most officers discounted or ignored this suggestion, contending that the Hawaiian Islands were well-nigh impregnable. Anyway, the "gun club" advocates argued, if the Pacific Fleet were in port during such an attack its guns would augment the defenses of the land bases to such a great extent that any such foolhardy attack would be beaten off.

The December 7, 1941, attack differed only in minor details from the simulated attacks of eight and nine years earlier. Commander Ramsey's prophecy came true.

The handful of United States aircraft carriers which were operating with the fleet that fateful day were spared to form the nucleus of a new navy which had to be rebuilt to meet the gigantic task it faced after December 7. Pearl Harbor demonstrated beyond question the vulnerability of surface ships from attack by airplanes. For those who may still have doubted, the sinking of the HMS *Prince of Wales* and HMS *Repulse* a short time later drove home this lesson. Thus, the aircraft carrier became the new "Queen of the Seas." It has not yet relinquished this title nor doubtless will it in the foreseeable future.

Throughout the Pacific War, the aircraft carrier was to prove invaluable in every operation. Complete command of the air was essential for amphibious or hit-and-run assaults. Carrier aircraft provided this. Fast carrier task forces which spearheaded every Pacific assault became known throughout the world as "the fleet that came to stay."

It was with a carrier task force that Admiral Halsey took the initiative for the first time in the war, with a strike against the Marshall and Gilbert Islands in February, 1942. At the same time, the Japanese used their carriers to maintain air superiority, and continued to make one conquest after another in the Far East and southwestern Pacific.

It was inevitable that both carrier forces soon would clash head on. This happened on May 8, 1942, in the Coral Sea. For the first time opposing fleets did not exchange gunfire. Only the antiaircraft guns of the defending ships saw action. Offensive attacks on both sides were by aircraft. The United States lost the USS *Lexington*, Japan lost the carrier *Shoho*. The Japanese drive to the south was checked for the first time. Soon afterward, a western thrust by the Japanese ended at Midway. Admiral Spruance was responsible for turning the tide of war. The attacking Japanese fleet was shattered with the loss of four more carriers, *Kaga*, *Akagi*, *Soryu*, and *Hiryu*. The USS *Yorktown* was sunk. Again the battle was waged principally by opposing aircraft.

From this point on, the United States was on the offensive. This westward drive of the American forces was slow until the arrival in 1943 of the newest class of American carrier, the *Essex*. The twenty-four ships of the *Essex* class not only provided the backbone of the World War II carrier force, but a quarter of a century later these ships still remain active in the modern Navy. They are slowly being replaced as attack carriers due to the size of modern jet aircraft, but it is anticipated that the venerable *Essex*-class carriers will be on duty in antisubmarine warfare missions for many, many years to come.

The *Essex*-class carriers made possible the island-hopping strategy in the Pacific. The drive across the central Pacific began as soon as the carrier strength was sufficient. First Tarawa, then Majuro, Kwajalein, and Palau were taken by amphibious operations conducted under an umbrella of Navy and Marine Corps aircraft operating from these carriers. Truk, the Japanese Pearl Harbor of the central Pacific, was attacked and bypassed to wither and die as the war forged westward across the Pacific.

Admiral Raymond A. Spruance, whose Fifth Fleet was the naval backbone and nerve center for the central Pacific offensive from Tarawa to Okinawa, captured the Marianas and broke the back of Japanese carrier air strength in the Battle of the Philippine Sea. Never again were the Japanese able to mount any appreciable aircraft carrier strength. The United States Fleet was able to cruise practically at will without threat of air attack, unless they came within the range of land-based aircraft defending the homeland islands.

So staggering was the loss of its aircraft carriers to Japan that it mobilized its surviving pilots into flying suicide squadrons in an effort to destroy American aircraft carriers and in that way even the military balance of force. Japanese suicide pilots often passed up easier targets in order to reach the aircraft carriers in the heart of the American task force. The kamikaze—"Divine Wind"—flew regular attack aircraft of any type or specially built "Baka" bombs. The Bakas, carried under a twin-engine plane, were released high above the target so that they could glide down upon it. The winged bomb was piloted on its one-way mission. These pilots, and those flying regular aircraft on kamikaze missions, could only hope to take many of the enemy with them when they plunged headlong into the target. The suicidal kamikaze took a terrific toll of United States ships, but it did not slow the westward march to victory.

In the face of this determined, suicidal defense, American forces attacked and ultimately captured bitterly defended Iwo Jima and Okinawa as a prelude to a planned operation against the homeland of Japan. In the later months of World War II, carrier aircraft, joined by long-range bombers flying from island bases wrested from the Japanese, struck the homeland empire almost with impunity. The war ended before an amphibious assault upon Japan itself was necessary.

The American aircraft carrier achieved great success in World War II. In postwar years, as the nation's military responsibilities broadened, the aircraft carrier has become the workhorse of the cold war.

Carrier task forces are constantly on station in the Mediterranean as the center of the Sixth Fleet, which has a considerable stabilizing influence on the mid-Eastern and European section of the world. The Sixth Fleet, by its mere presence, has proven its ability to deter or control conflict. The Mediterranean location is strategic because all peninsular Europe is within reach of carrier aircraft based in Mediterranean waters.

In the western Pacific, the Seventh Fleet is also built around the aircraft carrier, which has proven its worth as a ready substitute for overseas bases at crucial moments in history. Certainly this was the case in Korea when the hordes of Communists swept down the peninsula almost to its tip, destroying everything in the way. When United Nations forces intervened to stop the onslaught, Seventh Fleet carriers, floating self-contained air bases, were the only American airports available to the defenders during those, the darkest days of Korea. Later, carrier task forces offered United Nations forces ashore much of their air cover and support in attacking enemy targets north to the Yalu River.

Again, when the cold war turned hot in Vietnam, the President turned to the Navy's attack carrier-borne squadrons when precise, measured response was demanded. In both shooting wars of the mid-century, it was the Navy who showed the way in precision, dive-bombing attacks.

The evolution of the aircraft carrier has led to construction of the nuclear-powered *Enterprise*, a ship which epitomizes the state of the art of naval aviation. The *Enterprise* displaces 85,350 tons, with an overall flight-deck length of more than 1,100 feet. Some 250 feet wide

—almost as wide as a football field is long—the huge ship is home for nearly 4,600 men who fly and maintain the squadrons of aircraft embarked. They form a completely self-contained community. Powered by eight nuclear reactors generating a total of 200,000 horsepower, the *Enterprise* can move at more than 30 knots. Her speed, plus the long range of her aircraft, enables her range of influence to cover hundreds of thousands of square miles in any single day.

With the use of naval tactical data systems installed in all new carriers and coordinated with high performance radars, the *Enterprise* can automatically track hundreds of targets at any one time. The antiaircraft missiles of the screening vessels in a carrier task force can destroy attacking aircraft in the order of the threat which they pose to the force. Target selection is done automatically by radar-fed computers tracking the targets. Gone are the days when ships were forced to limit their attention to one or two incoming aircraft and defend themselves with barrages of thousands of antiaircraft gun bullets. Computerized antiaircraft defense systems are predicated upon one missile for one plane killed. Through airborne early-warning devices, targets are discovered a hundred miles or more away. Intercepts may begin immediately.

In addition to mobility, the aircraft carrier force also features versatility of attack weapons. Aircraft deployed aboard Navy carriers today have a choice of up to twenty different types of weapons with which to press home an attack.

By contrast to the night in June, 1944, when the American commander courageously ordered his ships to "turn on the lights" so that pilots, never trained in night landings, could be saved upon returning after dark from an especially long-range strike, flight operations now go around the clock as a matter of routine. Large carriers also offer improved all-weather capabilities. Steam catapults launch a strike force of ninety planes, some weighing as much as 35 tons each, in less than fifteen minutes. Angled landing decks permit simultaneous recovery and launching of planes.

In an era when the United States faces a four-ocean challenge to national survival, the carrier task force offers an ideal weapons system to cover vast areas of the world with a minimum of expense in manpower or hardware. The carrier task force can project with precise direction and intensity the exact degree of force required. It can gain and maintain control of the air in any region of conflict. It provides close air support for troops ashore.

As has been repeatedly demonstrated, the attack carrier is an optimum weapons system for deterrence or successful prosecution of limited war. No weapons system in the foreseeable future can replace the deployed attack carrier with its manned aircraft in its limited-war role. Land-based aircraft cannot meet these needs without depending upon foreign bases which may not be available. Missiles cannot replace manned aircraft for limited war targets, for they are not discriminating enough; nor can they be recalled once they are launched.

Thus today's primary mission for the attack carrier force is to deter the Communists from domination of the free people of the world. But versatility gives the attack carrier force responsibilities all across the spectrum of warfare possibilities from cold war to general war.

In cold war, aircraft carrier task forces serve as a major instrument of national policy due to their unique capability to:

Maintain the freedom of the seas.

Encourage our allies by being deployed close to trouble spots, without the territorial and political complications which accompany land bases or without placing troops ashore.

Demonstrate our intention and capability to honor our commitments to our allies.

Act as ambassadors of goodwill in support of the people-to-people program.

"Show the flag" in ports of the world as a constant reminder that the United States Navy is a potent power for world peace.

Discourage acts of aggression which might lead to limited war.

Respond at once where disorders threaten peace as in the Suez, Lebanon, the Quemoys, Southeast Asia.

The influence of the deployed aircraft carriers to deter limited war may be brought to bear without foreign land bases, without infringing upon the sovereignty of Allied or neutral nations, without the vulnerability of fixed land bases, and without endangering the population of the United States or our allies. However, if limited war occurs, deployed aircraft carriers have the capability:

To respond promptly with ready forces.

To carry the war to the enemy's shores, projecting controlled United States power overseas, reducing to the minimum the risk of starting a general war.

To counter high-performance aircraft of enemy nations.

To maintain control of the air over the fleet and landing forces.

To support and protect amphibious landings, providing close air support to ground troops according to their demands.

To interdict enemy lines of communications.

To mount air attacks precisely tailored to the objective.

To defend itself against or elude attacks by aircraft, submarines, or missiles.

Some contend carrier forces could be vulnerable to missile attack.

It should be recalled here that early in World War II the aircraft carrier *Lexington* discovered that the best defense against high-level bombing attacks was to maintain a steady course until the bombs were actually seen to leave the attacking aircraft. At this point a radical turn put the ship where the bombs were not when they landed. Much the same type of elusive defense can be taken with long-range detection of missiles. But even here, the high-speed carrier task group must first be found before it can be attacked by planes or missiles.

Should general war occur, aircraft carriers can mount nuclear weapon attacks upon vital targets almost anywhere on the periphery of the Eurasian landmass. They may represent a major portion of our residual forces in the event of surprise nuclear attack, since carriers, with built-in defense against the shock of nearby water or airbursts of atomic weapons, have high survivability capability.

This deterrent second-strike capability of the aircraft carrier force is an added dividend to the United States security insurance policy.

⚓

CHAPTER EIGHT

The Navy–Marine Corps Team Wades Ashore

Amphibious warfare originated in the eastern Mediterranean, which was the crossroads of early ocean-borne commerce. Egypt, Phoenecia, Persia, Crete, Greece, and Rome all projected their armies into enemy territory via oar-powered craft.

In the Aegean Sea, Greece dominated the trade routes with her navy. When challenged by Corinth, a rising sea power, and by Sparta, Greece undertook to strike her enemies' colonies in Sicily, and the city of Syracuse in particular. After a three-year effort by the Athenian Nicias, the first large-scale amphibious enterprise was doomed to failure because of lack of logistic support.

Then Alexander the Great laid siege to the ancient city of Tyre. After seven months, using his triremes, quinqueremes, and ships carrying battering rams, he built a pier, breached the stone walls, and captured the city. He went on to conquer more worlds as the first great successful amphibious commander. Subsequently, Alexander extended his influence to cover the countries adjacent to the eastern Mediterranean area, including Egypt.

Against determined opposition Caesar used amphibious forces to invade England and for 500 years Roman influence dominated Britain's culture. Again in 1066, William the Conqueror invaded England by sea.

After World War I, the island nation of Japan embarked on a program of expansion, and she depended on her amphibious forces to capture parts of China. After Pearl Harbor she rapidly extended her Greater East Asia Co-Prosperity Sphere, using amphibious expeditions to conquer countries on a wholesale basis.

Rear Admiral Richmond Kelly Turner, Chief of War Plans for Admiral Ernest J. King, decided that the best way for the United States to stem the rising tide of Japanese aggression in the Pacific was to borrow their own technique of amphibious operations. He is to be credited with originating the modern concept of amphibious warfare. As World War II progressed westward in the Pacific, he became our foremost amphibious commander. He participated in most of the successful amphibious campaigns of both General Mac-Arthur and Admiral Nimitz in their westward march to victory in the Pacific. He was responsible for the development of many types of landing craft as well as modern underwater demolition teams.

The largest single amphibious operation was General Eisenhower's D-Day landing in Europe in June, 1944. General MacArthur's Inchon landing in the Korean conflict routed the North Korean army in the fall of 1950. He was thereby enabled to drive the North Koreans to the Yalu River before the entry of the Red Chinese into North Korea, which brought on a new war.

Unless we are willing to wait until this nation is invaded to fight for our freedom, we must be prepared to fight in the enemy's back-yard instead of our own. In order to fight there, we must be able to get there. We can do that only if we have the know-how and the vehicles to transport large numbers of troops and their equipment across the oceans. Once there, we must be able to place them ashore in the face of strong opposition and to maintain the flow of supplies needed to keep them there.

These are the responsibilities of the Navy—Marine Corps amphibious team. It has been the mission of the Navy and Marines since the Revolutionary War. Sailors and Marines who were with George Washington when he crossed the Delaware River to capture Trenton on Christmas Eve, 1776, had been conducting amphibious operations for almost a year. It was on March 3, 1776, that a force of 220 Marines and 50 seamen made the first United States sea-to-shore assault—a raid on Nassau in British Bahama Islands. Since that time, there have been more than one hundred major amphibious operations staged by American forces in all areas of the world. They range from the 1805 capture of the Derne fortress in Tripoli and the 1856 Indian skirmishes near Seattle, Washington, to the most extensive amphibious operations of all times—those of World War II. These were climaxed by the invasion of Europe in 1944 and the assault upon Okinawa, the latter being the most complex sea-to-shore evolution in the history of the world, because of the tremendous distances units had to travel to reach their ultimate destination.

The modern amphibious operations of World War II, Korea, and those afterward differ greatly from any landing made prior to World War II. Just as Washington crossed the Delaware in a longboat, early-day assault troops were carried ashore in any convenient craft, usually the ships' boats, ill-equipped to attack defended beaches. There were no special landing craft. Neither bluejackets nor Marines were given specialized amphibious warfare training. There was no special equipment, nor any special amphibious warfare tactics or manuals. It is small wonder that any amphibious assaults were successful, but they were.

The most significant success of the nineteenth century was the landing of a battalion of Marines at Guantanamo Bay, Cuba, during the Spanish-American War. Between the 1898 Guantanamo landing and August, 1942, when Marines stormed ashore at Guadalcanal in the South Pacific, there had been little call for American amphibious assaults. During World War I, United States troops arrived in France and unloaded alongside docks to the tune of welcoming bands. It was not until they were well established on the mainland that they came in contact with the enemy. Although it did not involve Yankee troops, one World War I amphibious landing should be mentioned, because of its negative impact upon military thinking in this nation and throughout the world.

In April, 1915, British and French naval forces placed five divisions of troops ashore on the Turkish peninsula of Gallipoli. The initial assault, although it was opposed, was successful. That success was short-lived, however. Provisions to supply the troops ashore were woefully inadequate. Units ashore were not coordinated. Communications collapsed. After eight months of fighting, during which 50,000 lives were lost, the surviving British and French forces were evacuated. Allied observers, including many Americans, believed that Gallipoli proved beyond all doubt that well-defended land areas could not be captured by an assault from the sea. This attitude prevailed in many areas until the World War II assault upon the Pacific atoll of Tarawa, where the Japanese had boasted that a million Marines could not dislodge them in a hundred years.

The confident Japanese had not counted upon the years of preparation which the United States Marines made for that fateful assault in the mid-Pacific. It was the threat of an explosively emerging Japan which concerned Navy–Marine Corps strategists after World War I. How could American forces reach far across the broad Pacific Ocean, maintaining lines of communications, if called upon to wage war with a nation that was acting more and more aggressive in consolidating its power among Asiatic nations?

The only answer was amphibious operations in an island-hopping strategy. In 1923, Marine Commandant John Lejeune pointed out that "on both flanks of a fleet crossing the Pacific are numerous islands suitable for submarine and air bases. All should be mopped up as progress is made."

It was not until a full decade later, however, that the Fleet Marine Force, especially designed for this purpose, came into being and rudimentary doctrine was evolved for amphibious warfare. During the years immediately preceding Pearl Harbor, the Navy and Marine Corps fought an uphill battle in order to train for amphibious war. No one else seemed interested. At the outbreak of the war, we still had much to learn. A few World War I destroyers had been converted to attack transports, and other transport duties had been assigned to inadequate merchant-type vessels. Close air support, heavy shore bombardment, underwater demolition, amphibious vehicles, all techniques commonplace today, were in their infancy or yet to be born in 1941. Yet, within four years, sea-to-shore assaults were developed into a science whose crowning achievements were the invasion of Normandy on D-Day and the assault upon Okinawa.

Normandy was the largest sea-to-shore operation the world has ever known. In sheer size, it may never again be equaled. More than two and three-quarters of a million people participated in the single invasion. The men were moved and protected by a fleet of more than four thousand ships and by some fifteen thousand aircraft.

While the Normandy landing was staged across the narrow English Channel, the assault upon Okinawa was staged across the largest body of water in the world, the Pacific Ocean, covering more than a third of the earth's surface. This final amphibious landing of World War II was the most complex ever attempted and should be considered the ultimate test of United States amphibious doctrine. Approximately 550,000 Allied troops took part. More than 50,000 of these were put ashore on D-Day after traveling from Australia, Hawaii, and the United States to this western Pacific rendezvous. Men and supplies, loaded in hundreds of ships whose speeds ranged from 8 to 28 knots, had to arrive off the shores of Okinawa with stopwatch precision. Combatant ships, "softening up" the target and attacking the nearby mainland of Japan, had to coordinate their movements with the invasion timetable—which had been put into motion weeks before when ships began leaving staging points for the date with H-Hour, April Fool's Day, 1945. There was no turning back, even in the face of suicidal waves of 1,900 kamikaze aircraft which sank 26 ships and damaged 164 more. The schedule was met.

The strategy for these amphibious operations of the Atlantic and Pacific wars had been conceived by the Navy–Marine Corps team in the mid-1930's. It matured on the bloody shores of Tarawa, the most costly of sixty-seven successful assaults made between Guadalcanal and victory just three years later.

The assault on Tarawa, which opened the central Pacific offensive, was one of the most bitter amphibious operations in history. Nine hundred and ninety Marines bought Tarawa atoll with their lives. Two thousand, three hundred and eleven others were wounded. Only eighteen of the more than 4,800 Japanese defenders survived the battle.

A tremendous price was paid for a piece of real estate only 800 yards wide and covering only four-tenths of a square mile in area. The investment in blood, however, advanced greatly the Central Pacific island-hopping timetable. The Pacific War was shortened by months.

Just as important were the lessons learned in amphibious warfare, expensive lessons which had to be experienced regardless of cost. Countless thousands of Americans are alive today because of the sacrifices made by the Marines of Tarawa. The lessons in pre-invasion bombardment, in underwater reconnaissance, in actual assaults upon beaches, and effective consolidation of positions and mopping up were used effectively to cut dramatically losses on the beachheads of Normandy, Saipan, Leyte, southern France, Iwo Jima, Sicily, Okinawa, and half a hundred other strategic locations throughout the world.

The amphibious capability of the United States has thus remained an important military factor in the years since World War II. During the Korean War, an amphibious assault at Inchon contributed decisively to the success of a drive northward by United Nations forces. Another major amphibious assault at Wonsan also achieved its objective. On July 18, 1958, Fleet Marine Forces afloat with the United States Sixth Fleet in the Mediterranean Sea responded to a plea for help from the civil-war-threatened Lebanese government. Within a few hours of the call, five thousand combat-ready Marines landed at Beirut without incident. During the Cuban crisis in the fall of 1962, amphibious forces of the United States Second Fleet, reinforced by similar units from the First Fleet in the Pacific, were marshaled in Florida waters, prepared to conduct large-scale amphibious assaults by sea and by air if required. Fleet Marine Forces of the Seventh Fleet were among the first reinforcements to be called into Vietnam as the war there escalated.

Short of all-out thermonuclear war, military actions in the foreseeable future are expected to follow the pattern of recent years— deterrence, local uprisings, protracted guerrilla activity, and limited "brush-fire" wars of varying degrees. The proper antidote for any of these is the deliberate, discriminating use of amphibious power. The presence of a highly trained combat force some six thousand yards off the shores of a troubled land could be the key ingredient for stability. Landing troops can prevent a shooting situation from developing. Should shooting start, these troops would be the best insurance against escalation of an incident into a war of magnitude.

And, finally, should a brush-fire or otherwise limited war flare up, the amphibious assault forces would be the first "firemen" to arrive on the scene to contain it until additional troops could be mobilized to defeat the enemy.

If a "fire brigade" is to be effective in extinguishing or containing a fire, it must be mobile, readily available with almost instantaneous reaction time. For this reason, the hard-core United States amphibious strength is constantly at sea, deployed on a global scale, in constant readiness. This element of sea power is ever on the move as it is drawn daily toward the most inflammable trouble spot of the day. The Navy–Marine Corps has provided the forces for immediate response in the past and will continue to do so in the future. Their trade is the amphibious assault, one of the most difficult and complex tasks of modern warfare.

There are six basic phases of any amphibious assault: (1) planning and training; (2) loading ships; (3) sea movement to assault areas; (4) pre-landing softening of assault targets; (5) D-Day, the initial sea-to-shore phase in which the Navy–Marine Corps team "walks" ashore; (6) establishment of the beachhead on a permanent basis.

Planning and training are essential factors of any military operation. Assault forces must be prepared for any contingency. This can be accomplished only by skillful planning well in advance of an actual landing. In addition, an assault force is in a constant state of training, for, like any team, it must practice constantly if it is to maintain peak efficiency. The Silver Strand of Coronado, California; the Onslow Beach of North Carolina; and the shores of the Mediterranean, Formosa, the Caribbean, and Hawaii are assaulted repeatedly as the Navy–Marine Corps team constantly sharpens skills and techniques. This never-ceasing training has made the amphibious team ready to go anywhere, anytime, at a moment's notice.

The second phase of an amphibious operation also takes place before a single man or ship leaves friendly shores. This is the combat loading of men and equipment into ships which will carry them to the assault targets. Every nook and cranny of a ship must be utilized efficiently, but even more important than full utilization of space is the orderly discharge of supplies for delivery to the beach. This is determined at this point. Failure to look ahead to the period of unloading tended to put the cart ahead of the horse. Troops successfully making the sea-to-shore transit may find themselves equipped with fancy field kitchens but no food, and mortars without ammunition. Items needed first must not be on the bottom of the load. Weapons, supplies, equipment, personnel must be loaded into ships so that they can arrive and be off-loaded in the order of priority demanded on the beachhead.

Unit integrity also must be preserved at all costs. Men and their equipment should not be separated into different ships. Loss of one ship in a convoy cannot be allowed to destroy the effectiveness of the human and material cargoes of the other ships in the attack force. Each amphibious assault ship should be a complete unit within itself.

The third phase of an amphibious operation is the sea movement of troops and material to the assault area. This is a Navy effort involving precise and coordinated navigation. Timing is essential. Units must converge upon the target from several different staging areas, but all must arrive in accordance with a strict timetable. During the sea movement of troops, the Navy is responsible for the protection of the landing force from enemy air, surface, or submarine attack.

Initial activity in the assault area itself marks the opening of the fourth phase of the operation—pre-assault softening of the landing areas. High-speed carrier photographic planes sweep the target to record gun and troop emplacements, airfields, beach conditions, barricades, and anything else recordable by cameras. Frogmen slip silently from submarines to reconnoiter beach approaches. Obstructions are charted and on the eve of H-Hour underwater demolition teams return to destroy these hazards to assault-wave craft.

Underwater reconnaissance and demolition were among the many lessons of Tarawa. Aerial photography and the memories of former residents of the atoll could not adequately establish the height of the reefs and the amount of clearance the boats would have. The estimates proved fatal to hundreds. Planners drafting the invasion of Europe recognized that the first line of German resistance would be mines and underwater obstacles to stop invasion craft. Underwater demolition teams were established quickly to clear these obstacles. An intensive training program was devised on the theory than a man is capable of ten times the physical output he normally believes possible. The Navy's UDT swimmers proved the point. Grueling night-and-day exercises in the Florida Everglades produced a Navy man accustomed to mud, noise, exhaustion, all types of hostile things—human and otherwise—and capable of swimming great distances, destroying anything in his path. These Navy frogmen opened the gateways to France despite losses of 60 to 70 per cent on "Omaha" Beach. Applying the lessons of Normandy, underwater demolition teams became standardized in the Pacific campaigns and losses were reduced to only one per cent.

The actual softening of the target is achieved through aerial and ship bombardment. Again Tarawa proved to be an effective teacher. Limited cruiser bombardment before D-Day and an early-morning round of fire by battleships before H-Hour hardly fazed the well-entrenched defenders. Nothing is more destructive and demoralizing to an enemy than continuous pounding from bombarding warships maintaining the pressure hour after hour, around the clock, for days on end if needed, and augmented by air strikes which may include bombs, strafing, fire attacks, and a variety of other types of weapons attacks. Bombardments of atolls—attacked after Tarawa—left little alive above ground. Even vegetation was disintegrated. Eniwetok, for example, appeared little different after a pre-landing bombardment than it did years later after an atomic bomb test.

Essential to any preinvasion activity is complete control of the air in the vicinity of the target. This must be accomplished before any other overt step is taken. Once air superiority is established by Navy carrier forces, it must be maintained throughout this phase of an amphibious operation and during the subsequent landing and consolidation of the beachhead and until the Seabees have shore-based facilities ready to handle aircraft.

H-Hour—the actual movement of troops from sea to shore is the next to the last phase of an amphibious operation. If the previous four phases are successful, the actual assault should go smoothly.

Most dramatic progress has been made since World War II in the assault portion of the amphibious operation because a new dimension has been added through the use of helicopters. Marines experimented with autogiros in the 1932 Nicaraguan campaign, during which they also unveiled dive-bombing and close air support, but helicopters were not really needed until nuclear weapons forced dispersal of amphibious fleets. Since then, the doctrine of vertical envelopment has been established. The "choppers" have proven quick and efficient in moving initial assault waves ashore. They can bypass poor landing beaches. They can open pincer attacks by flying over or around enemy beach defense in order to close in from the rear while boats laden with assault forces attack from the front. Where absolute surprise is essential, helicopters could "hit the beach," while attacking amphibious forces are still over the horizon. Once the first wave is delivered and the initial beachhead is established, the "whirlybirds" are ideal for tactical operations; communications; and ferrying supplies, wounded, and replacements. In short, helicopters have proven their capacity for tactical surprise and versatility through their mobility and speed.

While the helicopter is effective in isolating specific targets or moving troops ashore in a major invasion, it is still only one of two ways to put troops and their equipment on the beach. We must again look to the sea for movement of any volume of men and material such as is needed to make an amphibious operation successful.

LPH's—Amphibious Assault Ships—are recently developed helo-carriers which are home not only for the helicopters but also the two thousand combat-ready and equipped Marine landing team they will ferry ashore. These carriers may operate as the center of a small assault force or may be included in a major invasion fleet.

LPD's—Amphibious Transports, Dock—are to small boats and amphibious personnel carriers and tanks what the LPH's are to helicopters. The LPD leaves port with fully loaded landing craft in their deep, voluminous belly. Upon arrival at the assault area, the well-deck is flooded and the equipment and troop-laden litter of small craft sail into the ocean on its way to the beach.

LST's—Landing Ships, Tank—are the cumbersome but versatile

87

workhorses of the amphibious fleet which were known as "large slow targets" among those who sailed them during World War II. LST's may deliver their cargo of men and material directly upon the beach, unloading through huge hinged and ramped bows. They can unload amphibious tractors, tanks, and personnel carriers directly into the sea. They can be converted into machine shops, hospitals, or any of a dozen or more special types of craft needed in an amphibious operation. New models are being built with a 20-knot capability.

APA's and AKA's—Attack Transports and Attack Stores Ships, respectively—are specially constructed to carry the major volume of assault forces moved to the target area. They are unloaded at sea, with most of the cargo moved to the beach by small boats.

LVT's—Landing Vehicle, Tracked—are the amphibious landing craft capable of swimming across open waters, climbing coral reefs and other obstructions, and crawling over land at speeds of up to thirty miles an hour.

LCVP's—Landing Craft, Vehicle and Personnel—are the traditional flat-bottomed, blunt-bowed landing craft originally developed during World War II. These small boats are the primary means of unloading APA's and AKA's because their straight sides and open tops make them easy to load alongside a ship. They also may run up on the beach, drop front ramps, disgorge troops, vehicles, or supplies, back away from the shore, and return for more loads.

These are the principal types of many craft whose only function is to move the troops in the ship-to-shore phase of the amphibious operation.

When the troops hit the beach, the sixth phase commences. This is the fighting on land to establish and maintain a permanent beachhead. It is at this point that the Navy–Marine Corps team becomes truly three dimensional—sea, air, and land. Close air support and close gunfire support from ships provide troops ashore with the heavy artillery needed in any land battle. Ships and aircraft can strike targets only a short distance in front of advancing frontline infantrymen. As one rifleman with considerable frontline experience

88

The superliner SS United States *as she leaves New York on another crossing to Europe, passing the Statue of Liberty. (United States Lines)*

Automation is one of the American Merchant Marine's answers to the need of cutting operating costs to compete in world markets. SS Mormacargo is first fully automated ship to sail under the U.S. flag.

Close-up of the "containerized" deck load aboard the American President liner President Lincoln.

The nuclear-powered ship Savannah. *(MSTS photo)*

Replenishment under way has greatly reduced the dependence of American fleets upon advanced bases. Here, USS Truckee *refuels USS* Valley Forge.

Just as underway fueling extends the range of aircraft carriers, in-flight fueling from carrier-based tankers extends range of striking aircraft.

The nuclear-powered USS Enterprise, *largest warship in the world. Manned by a crew of 4,600, she is home for more than 100 aircraft.*

Spearheading an amphibious assault is a force dock landing ship and an amphibious assault helo-carrier with the attack cargo ship in the center.

The nerve and communications center of an amphibious operation is an amphibious command ship such as the USS Taconic.

The USS Churchill County, with huge doors in its bow, can deliver troops and equipment directly on the beaches.

The USS Fort Snelling is a dock landing ship whose primary mission is to move troops, heavy equipment, and the landing craft required to take them to the assault beaches.

Close to the shore, amphibious personnel carriers move out through the giant bow doors of the tank landing ship.

The Lykes Seabee barge and intermodal carrier. (J. J. Henry Co., Inc.)

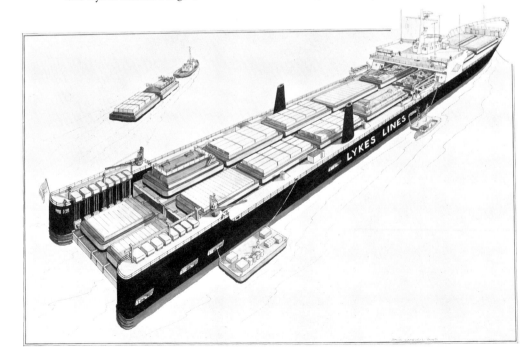

When Seabees line up for inspection or review they are just as apt to man "cherry pickers" as military weapons.

The antisubmarine hunter-killer squadron comprised of aircraft, surface ships, and submarines is the principal weapon the United States has against an undersea threat.

The "hedgehog" patterns send twin circles of destruction into the depths in which the submarine lurks.

The Project Apollo tracking-communication ship USNS Redstone *makes a high-speed run during her initial sea trials. (General Dynamics)*

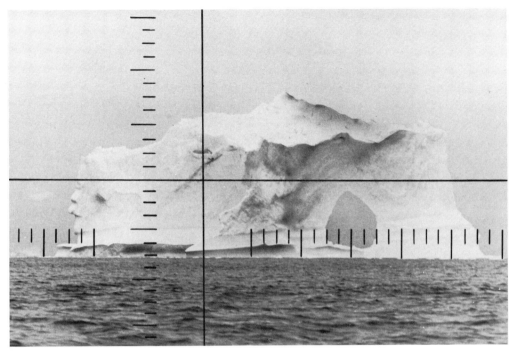

The USS Seadragon's *polar voyage periscope view of an iceberg.*

The explosive power hidden in the section of the USS John Marshall *just behind the conning tower exceeds all that unleashed during World War II.*

The Flip Ship, here in the process of standing on its tail, is a floating instrument platform 355 feet long.

Star I *crawls along the bottom of the sea. This is an experimental one-man research submarine.*

The Deep Quest, *a 50-ton research submarine designed to go to 6,000 feet.*

The 50-foot Aluminaut *is designed to operate to depths of 15,000 feet.*

Her twin nuclear reactors give USS Long Beach *a maximum range of 720 nautical miles a day — day after day.*

The nuclear guided-missile destroyer leader USS Bainbridge, *with her high clipper bow, has twin missile launchers fore and aft.*

The USS Chicago, a guided-missile cruiser. Converted from a World War II cruiser, she is powered by conventional oil-fueled engines.

Prototype of a newer, faster class of LST (Landing Ship Tank).

Drawing shows new construction design of fast combat support ship.

Sikorsky aircraft S-64 helicopter lifts container from forward section of Container Despatcher, owned by American Export Isbrandtsen Lines, before carrying it ashore. (Sikorsky Aircraft)

Hawkeye, *one of the Navy's newest additions to carrier operations, is a turbo-prop aircraft.*

The hydrofoil research ship Plain-view *has a crew of 20.*

The SKMR-1, a hydroskimmer which hovers one and a half feet above the surface — ground or water.

The U.S. Coast Guard's "ship of the future," the 378-foot Cutter Hamilton. *(U.S. Coast Guard Photo)*

Wearing new battle grey paint over her former white coat is the 82-foot U.S. Coast Guard Cutter Point Young *on coastal surveillance patrol off South Vietnam. (U.S. Coast Guard Photo)*

commented: "If you don't get in a hole or down as flat on your belly as you can, you're mighty likely to get your backside full of arrows."

The finest precision has been achieved through close air-support missions using carrier-based Marine pilots who have had infantry experience so they can appreciate personally the ground situation. In close support of seasoned ground troops, Marine air squadrons routinely hit targets within fifty yards of front lines, in daylight or in darkness. Reliable and instantaneous communication is the key to this success. In close air support, the frontline commander has complete control over the aircraft, personally directing the strikes by radio. Aircraft may attack with napalm, high-velocity antipersonnel rockets, antitank rockets which are also deadly against bunkers and pillboxes, fragmentation bombs, general-purpose bombs of up to five hundred pounds in size, or they may strafe with guns.

In such an attack, planes are on station within minutes after the call for assistance. Control is transferred to the frontline commander, and on call the aircraft sweep over the target. Seconds after the final run, ground troops may move forward to exploit the fullest effect of the air attack. Ground commanders can order a dummy run over the target to keep the enemy tied down while the ground attack is launched.

Elsewhere on the beach, the consolidation of the beachhead continues. Specially trained Navy teams direct the continued flow of men and materials, evacuate the wounded and prisoners, and repair damaged equipment. At sea, the invasion fleet stands by for continued support, carrier task forces maintain essential air superiority, and surface ships prevent delivery of reinforcements to the enemy.

These, in brief, are the elements of an amphibious operation. The composition of the amphibious team depends upon many factors, most of which are determined months before the actual assault. This determination is made by answering dozens of questions, such as: "Is the nuclear threat of the enemy sufficient to prevent massing of ships?" "Do nearby enemy reserves make surprise essential?" "Can the target be isolated and taken leisurely?" "What will the tides be at the moment the first wave leaves for the beach?" "What obstacles will there be facing the landing craft?" "Where are the biggest guns of defending troops?"

If the correct answers have been given to these and other questions —Has the planning and training been adequate? Has the air–sea bombardment been sufficient? Were the proper mixtures of ships and aircraft, weapons and manpower, landing vehicles and materials on hand?—then and only then will the assault be successful.

With mobility the key to future amphibious operations, the Navy–Marine Corps team continues its quest for even better ways of extending the long reach of sea power across the beaches and inland. Ultimately this search could lead to seagoing paratroopers, operating from carrier-based transport planes. Or, it could mean undersea Marine guerrilla raiders spirited ashore in substantial numbers from submarines. And, while we look over the sea and under the sea for new ways of placing fighting men ashore on hostile lands, we must also look on the sea. The state of the art of waterborne amphibious vehicles continues to improve with developments, such as the ground-effects machine which can sweep over open seas, swamps, sandbars, and solid land at speeds of 50 to 70 knots.

Amphibious operations were built upon a foundation established long before the advent of nuclear weapons. The atomic bomb almost put American amphibians out of business, as preoccupation of our defense establishment with a strategy of massive deterrence for a period in mid-century decimated amphibious forces. Later, however, it was realized that humanity-destroying missiles are helpless against guerrillas and useless in meeting tactical situations. Regardless of the nature of war, one basic fact prevails:

Military might can destroy a land by remote control, but it can never control it. Areas can be controlled only with combat-trained and equipped troops on the ground. In order to control any region, a nation must have the capability of gettings its troops there and maintaining them for an indefinite period. The United States has this capability in its Navy–Marine Corps amphibious team.

American amphibious doctrine thus has proven itself sufficiently flexible to survive even in a nuclear age. This nation today has recognized the need for a mobile force in readiness, prepared to land at any of the world's trouble spots should the need arise.

Hence, the Navy–Marine Corps team plays a major role in a policy of graduated deterrence through which this country hopes to contain conflicts before they explode with an atomic mushroom. Should general nuclear war occur, however, the survivability of the amphibious forces embarked in warships under way and dispersed over broad expanses of ocean will make them one of the few military ground forces surviving intact. This force could ensure ultimate victory for the free world.

⚓

CHAPTER NINE

"Can Do!"

Synonymous with amphibious warfare is a strange breed of sailor who knows little about ships, fights like a Marine, and can build almost anything from an airfield to a washing machine.

The Seabees, a product of World War II, have built in a very few years a legend about their ability to complete any construction job in record time, especially under fire. *Construimus, batuimus*— "We Build, We Fight"—is the formal motto of the Navy's Construction Battalions as the Seabees are known officially; but for those who have worked with the rough-and-tumble construction gangs wearing Navy blue, "Can do!" has become their most familiar nickname.

Before Pearl Harbor, the Navy used civilian contractors for most of its overseas building projects. Thousands of civilian construction workers were captured or slain on Guam, Wake Island, and the Philippines. These civilians were not trained to defend themselves under attack, and even if they had borne arms, it would have been at the risk of summary execution as guerrillas if captured.

Three weeks after Pearl Harbor, the Seabees were organized by Admiral Ben Morrell. Rugged construction workers were recruited and given brief but intensive military training by the Marine Corps. The first Seabee units were on their way to the South Pacific before the end of January, 1942. In the nearly four years that followed, the Seabees participated in every amphibious operation conducted by American fighting men—Army and Marine—including the crossing of the Rhine. Usually the Seabees carried equipment ashore with the first assault waves in order to establish immediately needed temporary bases of operation. In at least one instance, they were waiting for invading troops. When Marines hit the beaches of New Georgia, a fifty-year-old Seabee lieutenant commander, Robert L. Ryan, stepped from the jungle with the greeting, "It is always a pleasure to welcome the Marines." Ryan headed a Seabee group placed ashore ahead of D-Day to locate the best site for an airstrip. Construction commenced as soon as the landing forces arrived with the Seabees' tools.

Marines who landed at Eniwetok grumbled admiringly about the Seabees' cornering all the war trophies. Enterprising Seabees discovered that the best way to get war souvenirs was to move ahead of the front lines and capture enemy command posts themselves.

During the Korean War, the leathernecks pushing to Seoul after the Inchon landings rained small-arms fire on a train approaching the front lines until they realized that the train crew was a happy-go-lucky group of Seabees who somehow, somewhere had "liberated" the train from its North Korean owners.

The mutual admiration society which developed between the Marines and Seabees dates back to the early South Pacific landings of Guadalcanal where a Marine general complained that the Seabees were building roads so fast that the Japanese were using them for retreat. A World War II sign on a Marine jungle camp told the story poetically:

When we reach the Isle of Japan with our caps at jaunty tilt,
We'll enter the City of Tokyo on roads the Seabees built.

The close affinity between the Seabees and the Marines was invaluable because they had to work and fight side by side on all of the Pacific island beachheads. The Seabees built things with the same inventiveness, initiative, and esprit de corps with which the Marines fought. Seabee-built projects sometimes cost nothing except ingenuity and discarded material. Sometimes the projects ran into the millions. Bombproof diesel and fuel-oil storage plants were burrowed into the interior of mountains. Shipbuilding and ship repair facilities, port and harbor works, aviation training and operating stations,

93

ammunition depots and ordnance production facilities, supply depots, hospitals, fleet operating bases, fuel depots, housing, and floating docks of all sizes and shapes have been Seabee projects.

During World War II, Seabees constructed bases in the United Kingdom, Iceland, Newfoundland, Thule, Bermuda, the Caribbean, Panama, South America, Africa, Alaska, Hawaii, Midway, Wake, Guam, the Philippines, Samoa, and wherever else the fighting forces of this nation went in the Pacific. The total added up to more than four hundred advanced bases valued at more than $2,000,000,000. These bases accommodated as many as 50,000 men and contained industrial, hospital, storage, and other facilities required for cities several times that population. Eighteen Pacific bases had a project cost of 10 million dollars each. All but four had to be constructed on land which was first wrested from the enemy.

After it was all over, Fleet Admiral Ernest J. King, wartime commander in chief of the entire Navy, evaluated the Seabees in an official report: "The accomplishments of the Seabees have been one of the outstanding features of the war. . . ."

Admiral King emphasized that the Seabees proved especially adept at building airfields, pointing with pride to the fact that they could build or repair fields in any type of weather, hot or cold, faster than the enemy could damage or destroy them.

Construction of advanced bases was then, and is today, a complex task. The first job was to get the equipment ashore despite enemy opposition. After the beachhead was established, roads had to be cut inland to the site of the camp and airstrip. Access was critical and a premium was placed on speed. At Vella Lavella, Seabees roughed out nine miles of road the first day they hit the beach. Supplies and equipment had to be moved off the exposed beach area. Many other activities were undertaken simultaneously: a campsite was cleared and a source of water was found and developed; hospital and mess-hall facilities were set up; gun emplacements were built; the airstrip was started.

If an air base were cut out of virgin jungle, clearing the field usually was complicated by drainage and grading problems.

Because the airfield was necessary for protection of the base, maximum speed was demanded during early stages of construction. Seabees normally were able to complete a World War II fighter strip and have it operational in less than two weeks, and this time has been cut on some occasions to only four days. New "instant airfield" kits and techniques now have reduced the time to a matter of hours.

Once the job is completed and the planes are using the field, the Seabees' task is far from over. They must maintain it, repair it after attacks. On many occasions during World War II, bombed-out airstrips were repaired while American fighter aircraft, which had risen to meet the enemy, circled overhead waiting to land. In building and in repairing the airfield, time was of the essence and the success of the Seabees was spelled out by the ingenious ways in which they short-cut the time in an effort to finish the job "yesterday." For instance, Seabees knew that a bulldozer could knock over a tree, but this was too time-consuming, so they hooked steel cables between two bulldozers and swept up the field, "harvesting" all growth which stood in the path.

Seabee ingenuity put to work all discarded materials. Empty oil drums were a constant challenge. They cut out the ends and welded the drums into drainage pipes which they laid by the mile. They used drums for culverts, sewers, chimneys, shower baths, furniture, stoves, washing machines, and bathtubs, and rolled them out flat for walls and roofs, and even dock shoring. They cut them up for trusses, filled them with sand or coral for buttresses, and even used them for the hulls of canoes equipped with outriggers from Japanese seaplanes shot down by Marine or Seabee gunners.

In the Marshall Islands, an unpacked shipment of structural steel was found. Unable to read Japanese assembly directions, Seabees assumed it was a warehouse. Only after a thoroughly satisfactory warehouse had been built did they learn from an interpreter that it should have been an airplane hangar.

Seabees proved to be excellent defense troops under fire. Many were decorated. General MacArthur awarded the distinguished unit citation to the 40th Seabee Battalion for action against the enemy on Los Negros Island in March, 1944. Landing when the Army's dismounted cavalry units were struggling to hold their grip on a 200-foot

95

strip between Momote airstrip and Hyane Harbor, the Seabees drove bulldozers into the jungle to clear firelines for army guns. During the night, harassed by infiltrating enemy troops, they adopted infantry tactics for self-defense, scouting pockets of resistance and spotting pillboxes. The next morning, while the enemy was being pushed slowly back, they repaired the airstrip and built companion facilities.

It was the Seabees who made a "secret weapon" out of a bulldozer. With the dozer blade raised high as a shield, the Seabee driver charged enemy pillboxes. When they reached the target they merely dropped the blade and plowed the post under tons of dirt. After initial successes, the Navy armor-plated "dozer" blades for additional protection to drivers.

A group of Seabees, finding themselves the target of a Japanese airborne landing one midnight on Okinawa, threw down their tools and grabbed their carbines. By dawn they had killed or captured every one of the enemy and had saved the parked planes the enemy had come to destroy. With that, they calmly went back to work, putting the finishing touches on Okinawa's first airfield, completed by the Seabees in four short days.

Because their outstanding contribution clearly established the need for such a force, the Seabees were made a permanent part of the Navy in 1946. Continuing to show their aggressive know-how and "can do" attitude, the Seabees perform high-speed construction jobs for the Navy all over the world, ranging from the Arctic to the tropics and including all construction work at the South Pole.

Today there are two separate and distinct types of Seabee units which support an amphibious assault force: the Naval Amphibious Construction Battalion and the Naval Mobile Construction Battalion. Generally speaking, the Amphibious Construction Battalions are concerned with the ship-to-shore movement of troops and supplies. Mobile Construction Battalions are principally concerned with providing Marine air-and-ground units assault area construction support.

The pontoon causeway remains the principal means of rapidly moving ashore the heavy equipment and vast quantities of supplies required in an amphibious assault. The amphibious battalions maneuver the causeways into place and anchor them. Once located, the exposed causeways must be maintained constantly, even under enemy fire. This means the Seabees must fight wind, sea, and surf conditions as well as the enemy.

Amphibious Seabee battalions install bulk fuel lines to allow the rapid movement of fuel directly from tankers to the Marine Corps' assault fuel system ashore. These fuel lines may either be floated or laid on the bottom. Bottom-laid lines—30-foot lengths of 4½-inch oilfield casing—may be installed at a rate of a thousand feet an hour. Floating hoses are 4-inch-diameter lightweight gasoline discharge hose in 250-foot lengths. Special floater buoys keep the hose suspended two to three feet below the surface when filled with fuel. The job of removing damaged or inoperative landing craft, stalled vehicles, or any other equipment which impedes the rapid movement of equipment and supplies into the landing area is also a responsibility of the Seabees. The development and maintenance of supply areas, the construction and maintenance of roads—all are Seabee responsibilities. In short, the Seabees perform tasks required to ensure rapid and continuous movement of assault force men and equipment from the sea to their objective inland.

Engineering and construction support for the amphibious landing force is the responsibility of the Mobile Construction Battalions. Their tasks include the construction of the airfields and base facilities. Special mention should be given to airfields. Few areas of the world have fields capable of supporting heavy modern jet aircraft. These always are needed in a hurry for attack and fighter-defense purposes. The answer to this problem is the Marine Corps Short Airfield for Tactical Support, called SATS by the military. Fundamentally, this airfield consists of aluminum planking runway, taxiway, and parking apron. Catapults and arresting gear similar to those used on aircraft carriers allow launching and recovery of high-performance tactical jet aircraft. Shorter and narrower than the flight deck of the aircraft carrier USS *Enterprise*, SATS runways obviously need more than runways to sustain air operations. The task of constructing and maintaining navigation, ammunition, repair, and other logistical support facilities is the responsibility of the Seabee Mobile Construction Battalions.

The Seabees are unique among military organizations in that they are working constructively while they are training. In Southeast Asia, for instance, they built an airport in a short time when it was needed desperately by Thailand. A similar demand in Udorn resulted in the construction of a camp. In Guam, the Seabees mopped up after the devastating typhoon "Karen" and then settled down to the long-range rebuilding and rehabilitation program. In Greece, a vital communications link was developed to ensure an operational requirement in our own defense posture. Alaskans could only say "God bless the Seabees" after the Alaskan earthquake, when the construction forces started rebuilding hardly before the tremors stopped. They have worked, trained, and built projects in Laos, Thailand, Haiti, Ecuador, Africa, Okinawa, Chile, and Antarctica.

The Seabees' ability to construct public works in limited time under extremely adverse conditions and with only a handful of people has given the Navy builders a new role in the nation's people-to-people and counter-insurgency programs. They are, in fact, serving as a military peace corps. Seabee technical assistance teams, consisting of an officer who is a graduate engineer and a dozen or so specially trained enlisted personnel, are deployed in areas of Latin America, Asia, and Africa where host nations seek and need assistance in completing small community development projects. These may be a road, a library, a water system, a school, a reservoir, a sewer system, a well, anything of a community nature which needs the special attention of builders. Most of this work is done in outlying districts, in isolated towns, in the more poverty-stricken regions of the world where natives are particularly susceptible to the blandishments and terrorism of communism.

How has this experiment in people-to-people relations worked out? It has been an impressive success. The Navy men are building long-lasting projects for community good and at the same time are winning the battle for the hearts and minds of the people of these lands. Large numbers of American servicemen are going to work along with the people of the country, rolling up their sleeves with them. Most important, they are also teaching them something worthwhile, something that will raise the standard of living in their community, in addition to improving the community's health, sanitation, flood control, education, and general welfare. The Seabee technical assistance teams are putting something into the country. They are developing human resources. Such a contribution is valuable beyond description. Dollar for dollar, the technical assistance program has been called one of the best overseas investments this nation has ever made. These teams have earned high praise from officials of every country involved, for as one Asian host commented:

"This is the first time these people have ever seen a Caucasian work with his hands, and not only that but use his hands to help train their hands to do the job. It is fantastic what these people think and have in their hearts for those Seabees. They begged and cried for them not to leave this village."

Today's naval construction forces are carrying on as their predecessors did in World War II and fulfilling the motto "Can do!" and in most cases are accomplishing "the impossible today, with the miracles taking a day longer."

They are the fleet's military engineers, equipped to construct anything, anywhere in the world. In training they are working on projects which improve the United States image and defense posture and hopefully in this manner are serving to help prevent World War III.

In the event of war, limited or general, the role of the Seabees in an amphibious assault will determine the success of the operation, for the Seabees must provide and maintain the facilities required to provide the Marines with the weapons of war, the ammunition, the food, the supplies, and the tactical air support which is so critical to any such amphibious operation.

As integral parts of the amphibious assault force which has been called upon many times in Korea, South Vietnam, and elsewhere throughout the world, the Navy Construction Battalions are deployed constantly throughout the world, ready for instantaneous response.

Unlike any other military organization, however, the Seabees build while they train. In peacetime, they contribute to the development of

99

the free world. In wartime, they contribute to the preservation of that freedom.

Construimus, batuimus—We Build, We Fight—in peace and in war.

⚓

CHAPTER TEN

War Under the Seas

Successful prosecution of antisubmarine warfare may not ensure victory in any future war, but failure can only invite disaster.

This single sentence sums up the importance of the submarine to any oceanic power. The submarine has achieved a greater level of importance today than at any time in history. Not only is the submarine a primary weapon for use against military and commercial surface shipping, but it has assumed a variety of new cold-war and limited-war missions and, with the advent of Polaris, has become an invulnerable weapon of nuclear strategic deterrence.

Undersea craft have challenged man's ingenuity since the days of Alexander the Great. Alexander used a glass barrel for shallow-depth observations in the Mediterranean Sea. Later he used many such barrels to frighten away enemy ships at Tyre. Leonardo da Vinci, the genius of late medieval times, experimented with underwater vessels and sounding equipment. A later age found an inventive Dutch experimenter, Cornelius Van Drebbel, submerging for brief periods in a leather-covered rowboat operated by twelve oarsmen.

It took the Connecticut Yankee ingenuity of David Bushnell to develop the first effective submarine. His "Bushnell's turtle," a one-man submarine made of oak staves with iron bands like a stout brandy cask, is credited with driving a British fleet out of New York Harbor during critical early days of the Revolution. On the night of September 6, 1776, a certain Sergeant Lee set out with the personal blessings of General George Washington. His target was the HMS *Eagle*, flagship of the British fleet. A heavy covering of tar prevented

Lee from attaching a 150-pound powder charge to the flagship's wooden hull. When daylight forced Lee to withdraw, the British discovered the strange craft bobbing through the water. They gave chase in longboats. Lee released his cargo of explosives which drifted among the British boats before exploding with a tremendous roar and a tall spout of water. Chunks of the oaken bomb case rained down upon the British sailors. There was no damage, but the British followed the course of discretion rather than valor. They withdrew to safer anchorages which contained no diabolical craft such as the ponderous Turtle.

It was nearly a century later before a submarine sank a ship. At the outbreak of the Civil War, Union and Confederate forces embarked upon a race to develop an effective undersea craft. The South won, launching the submarine *H. L. Hunley*, on February 14, 1863. The cigar-shaped, hand-powered submarine had an ill-fated career before achieving a final burst of glory. Twice she foundered with the loss of all her crew of eight except for her skipper. The third time she sank, he drowned too. Raised once again, the *Hunley* attacked the USS *Housatonic*, blockading the Charleston Harbor. *Hunley's* torpedo was more like a mine or underwater bomb carried at the end of a long spar protruding from her nose. The explosion against the *Housatonic* not only gave the Union blockader the doubtful distinction of being the first ship sunk by a submarine, but it sank the *Hunley* as well. This time, the *Hunley* was down for keeps.

John P. Holland designed the first operational submarine as we know it today. His vessel had a gasoline combustion engine for surface travel and was battery powered for underwater maneuvering. The United States Navy acquired the USS *Holland* in 1900 to make tentative military probes under the seas, but it was Germany who forged ahead of the world in undersea warfare. By the time World War I began, the Kaiser's navy was ready to add a new under-the-sea dimension to naval warfare. Successes were immediate and dramatic. Early on the morning of September 22, 1914, a single German submarine, the *U-9*, sank three British cruisers, the HMS *Aboukir*, HMS *Cressy*, and HMS *Hogue*, in less than an hour's time.

For political and economic reasons, the Germans began indiscriminately sinking merchant ships without warning, a practice considered barbaric by the world at that time. The torpedoing of the proud British liner *Lusitania* with the loss of more than 1,000 people, including 124 Americans, was a tactical success, but a strategic blunder. This turned American public opinion against Germany. Continued submarine attacks against civilian shipping ultimately forced the United States into World War I against the Germans. Major naval efforts by the United States consisted of defensive measures against the submarines initiated by able American Admiral William S. Sims. These took a substantial toll. Allied surface ships sank sixty-five U-boats. Allied submarines accounted for another twenty. Mines sank seventeen in the North Sea. Even with these heavy losses, the Kaiser's submarine fleet almost spelled defeat for the Allies in World War I as did Adolf Hitler's undersea fleet in World War II.

After World War II, Winston Churchill, who had faced the horrors of Dunkirk, withstood the downpour of Nazi bombs and V-1 rockets, and knew of the deadly Allied-Axis race to achieve nuclear weaponry first, commented: "The only thing that ever frightened me during the war was the U-boat peril!"

Churchill knew that Allied victory hinged on keeping open the sea-lanes to Europe from North America. He knew that Hitler's submarines had to be stopped before any thought could be given to final victory.

With only a handful of submarines—fifty-seven at the outset—Germany had launched a World War II undersea offensive in the Atlantic which came close to bringing the Allies to their knees. Between 1939 and 1945, Axis U-boats sank 2,758 Allied merchant ships totaling more than 14,500,000 tons. On the night of April 3, 1941, a German wolf pack sank ten units of a 22-ship convoy, causing President Franklin D. Roosevelt to order United States naval ships to take up escort duties. Again the submarine threat was bringing the United States closer and closer to war.

The first American naval casualties of World War II were the torpedoing of the USS *Kearney* and USS *Reuben James* on Atlantic convoy duty in October, 1941. The *James* sank.

The blackest year of the Battle of the Atlantic was 1942. More than 1,000 ships left American shores and were sent to the bottom of the sea by Nazi torpedoes. An average of 73 German submarines prowled the Atlantic in wolf packs every day of that year in which Germany added 244 new boats to her fleet.

Antisubmarine warfare suddenly came of age. First, the convoy system was improved greatly with merchant ships protected by destroyers and aircraft during stormy voyages across the Atlantic. The effectiveness of radar and sonar, depth charges and torpedoes, was improved, but this was not enough to stem the tide. Admiral E. J. King, Commander in Chief of the United States Fleet, established the Tenth Fleet under his personal direction. Its sole function was to combat the Nazi submarines in the Atlantic. Antisubmarine forces took the offensive for the first time as a new hunter-killer doctrine was brought into being. Eleven aircraft carriers became the heart of hunter-killer task forces which stalked the U-boats throughout the Atlantic rather than wait for the wolf packs to strike. Fighter planes and bombers flying from the carriers tracked down the submarines when they were forced to surface for air. Air attacks with guns, depth charges, and bombs took a terrific toll. If the planes failed to get their quarry, hunter-killer destroyers moved in with depth charges and torpedoes. It was on one such an attack that a hunter-killer force under the command of Captain Daniel V. Gallery captured the German *U-505*, 150 miles off the American coast on June 4, 1944.

In 1941, the ratio of ships lost to submarines destroyed was 16 to 1. In 1942, the ratio dropped slightly to 13 to 1, but in 1943 with the hunter-killer offensive in full stride, a submarine was destroyed for every two Allied ships sunk. The following year, a Nazi U-boat was sent to the bottom for every merchant vessel lost. The tide had been changed in the Battle of the Atlantic.

Even with high losses, submarines proved an amazingly efficient weapon of war. It took relatively few submarines to impose substantial damage to surface ships. Hitler had, at the most, some 430 oceangoing boats manned by about 40,000 officers and men. The Allies had to build a surface force of twice that size and augment it with 2,200 aircraft before they could check the threat. In the Pacific War, 14 per cent of the United States Navy's World War II manpower sailed or supported fleet submarines which sank more than half of the Japanese shipping destroyed during the war. Of the 3,380,000 men and women wearing Navy blue during the war, only 16,000 actually manned the undersea fleet which destroyed more than 5,000,000 tons of Japanese merchant and military shipping, including the *Shenano*, the world's largest aircraft carrier, sent to the bottom on her maiden voyage outside Tokyo Bay.

At the end of World War II, the United States led the world in both submarine and antisubmarine operations. An overwhelming antisubmarine offensive finally reduced Atlantic losses to U-boats to an acceptable level. In the Pacific, American submarines operated without excessive losses in every corner of the ocean, even into the inland waters of the Nipponese homeland.

Competition between weapons systems and the defense against them is a never-ending struggle. Nowhere are the opposing sides of such a race more intertwined than in the battle under the sea. Technology is in a race against itself and science constantly strains to improve the stealth and deadliness of the submarine and at the same time strives to improve the ability to locate and destroy the menace which lurks silently in the depths of the oceans of the world. The battle rages between the hunter and the hunted.

Until 1955, the key to finding and destroying enemy submarines was dogging them until they were forced to surface for air and to recharge batteries. With the advent of nuclear power, however, the submarine no longer is a surface vessel able to dive under the sea for limited periods of time. The nuclear boat is a true submersible of unlimited endurance, performing better when submerged than when surfaced, maneuvering with the speed and agility of a surface craft, even though it is hundreds of feet under water. The unlimited stamina of nuclear submarines was demonstrated by USS *Triton's* underwater circumnavigation of the world. Their versatility is shown by excursions under the North Pole ice cap.

Nuclear power not only extends greatly the range of the submarine, but also complicates tremendously the problem of antisubmarine warfare. A World War II submarine, submerged for twenty-four hours, had an operating radius of 75 miles. In that same period, a submerged nuclear submarine has a cruising radius of 600 miles. The added mobility increases the potency of a submarine on the offensive and at the same time increases by sixty-four times the area which antisubmarine forces must search in following up a contact. The submerged speed of nuclear boats also exposes surface targets to attack from any direction. Slow-moving World War II submarines had to move into position along expected tracks of their prey, and wait patiently to attack from ahead. Defenders could concentrate protective screens in advance of convoys or fleets. A nuclear submarine now has the speed which allows it to hit from astern or from either flank as well as from ahead. Mandatory all-around protection will create a substantial drain of screening ships, always scarce in time of war.

In the contest between the submarine and antisubmarine forces, speed and endurance of nuclear boats now appear to give them the advantage over their opponents. This means that, at the moment, the nuclear submarine can pose a major challenge to control of the seas. That this potential is recognized by the Soviet Union is obvious from the fact that the submarine has become the backbone of Communist navies.

Admiral Sergei G. Gorshkov, Soviet Fleet Commander, has declared: "Tremendous concentration of striking power, unlimited range, high speed under water, great independence, great depth of submersion, and suitability for hidden action—all these and many more qualities of the new ships have to an unusual degree expanded the operative and combat capabilities of the submarine fleet which has now become the main striking force in a war at sea."

During the Battle of the Atlantic, the Soviet Union was on the receiving end of the North Atlantic sea-lanes, grumbling about shortages of supplies and the time it took Allied convoys to reach Murmansk. They watched as Nazi submarines sank Allied merchant ships faster than we could build them. They watched and learned. Today with six thousand free-world merchant ships on the high seas every day of the week, hauling more than 99 per cent of the free world's trade, including 85 per cent of the strategic goods used by the

United States, the four hundred Russian submarines would indeed be "the main striking force in a war at sea."

In addition to this traditional role of attacking enemy surface ships, both merchant and naval, the missions of the submarine have broadened greatly since World War II. Submarines are natural vehicles for delivery of guerrillas, underwater demolition and reconnaissance teams to hostile shores. Following the old saying, "Send a thief to catch a thief," submarines have been assigned primary roles in hunter-killer antisubmarine missions. Addition of nuclear ballistic missiles to undersea craft has given them major strategic deterrence responsibilities.

As the missions of the submarine forces of the world become more diverse, the importance of antisubmarine warfare increases at a similar pace. The United States Navy, moving to meet this threat from under the sea, has greatly improved its detection devices, extended the range and increased the efficiency of aircraft and helicopters, developed long-range submarine rockets and torpedoes, and modernized tactical procedures.

A good offense continues to be the best defense, and the hunter-killer task forces, instituted during World War II, remain the primary offensive response to the submarine challenge in this deadly game of hide-and-seek. Today the hunter-killer units are a tridimensional team of ships, planes, and submarines blended into a smoothly coordinated fighting unit. The keystone of the unit continues to be the aircraft carrier with its squadrons of helicopters and fixed-wing aircraft carrying the most modern detection equipment and antisubmarine weapons. These aircraft work closely with surface units and submarines to track down the enemy and bring him to bay.

They use a variety of techniques and electronic gadgets. Modern radar can detect the head of a periscope at great distances. Placing that radar in an aircraft can extend the range for many, many miles. Magnetic airborne detectors locate submarines below the surface by measuring disturbances of oceanic magnetism. Airborne "sniffers" can track down the wisp of exhaust fumes from the snorkel of conventional diesel-driven submarines. Effective ranges of underwater sound-detection equipment mounted on surface ships have been increased dramatically, but the distances at which enemy submarines may be located have been extended even more through the use of hunter-killer unit submarine and aircraft. The stealthy submarine, sailing below the effects of surface noises, offers an ideal long-range sonar listening platform. Sonobuoys are dropped from airplanes or "dunked" from helicopters to extend to hundreds of miles the listening and detection capabilities of the task force.

Long-distance weapons extend the range from which a kill can be made once the enemy is located. Homing torpedoes may be launched from ship or plane. Rocket-launched atomic depth charges and anti-submarine rockets extend a ship's lethal range for miles. Unmanned helicopters can be guided by remote control to target areas to deliver depth charges or launch torpedo attacks.

And so the contest continues.

The Communist navies have openly challenged the free world for domination of the seas. The race for control of these seas and the depths of inner space beneath their surface is on. To a large degree, victory will be determined by the effectiveness of submarine and antisubmarine forces.

⚓

CHAPTER ELEVEN

Polaris

The name Polaris has become a common word in the English vocabulary. It is not surprising, for the Polaris system is one of the most dramatic developments in the history of modern warfare. This revolutionary system was first conceived from the necessity for a near-foolproof strategic deterrent system.

One of the most ambitious scientific and technical battles ever waged by any United States military-industrial defense team brought Polaris into being. Two scientific achievements set the stage for the marriage of the ballistic missile and the submarine into a mobile, underwater strategic weapons system. First, nuclear power, only a dream until after mid-century, created a revolution in naval propulsion more dramatic than the change from sail to steam. Second, American industry, faced with the missile challenge of the Russian Sputnik, bulldozed a breakthrough in solid propellants for missiles.

As early as 1955, the Navy had started to wrestle with the problem of shipboard adaptability of ballistic missiles. After an initial effort to adapt the Army's short-lived Jupiter missile to seagoing purposes, the Navy cast aside all liquid fuels as too unstable and dangerous for use on rolling seas. Navy planners then embarked upon a new concept of solid-fueled missiles submarine-mounted.

This is one case where the Navy succeeded by putting all of its eggs in one basket. That "basket" was a new agency called, simply, "Special Projects." Under the able and dynamic leadership of imaginative and energetic Admiral William F. Raborn, Special Projects embarked upon the monumental task of building an all-new missile, constructing a huge submarine to carry the still untried weapon, and developing the myriad of electronic "black boxes" needed for under-sea navigation and missile control. The requirement that the Polaris submarine remain on station submerged for weeks at a time complicated the problem even further.

A nine-year timetable established by Raborn's Special Projects shop called for having the revolutionary Polaris operational in 1965. Instead, Admiral Raborn and his crew had the first Polaris submarine built, tested, and on patrol by November, 1960, less than four years after they first started designing the system. This remarkable feat was accomplished because of the untiring, dedicated efforts of hundreds of thousands of civilian and military men and women working for defense contractors, but a large measure of the success of Polaris can be attributed to the organizational wizardry of Admiral Raborn.

One of the most courageous decisions made by Raborn was to proceed independently with the development of missile, submarine, navigation, communications, and guidance systems, trusting that the pieces would all fit like a jigsaw puzzle when assembled in the submarine. Teamwork of previously unheard-of proportions was demanded because there were more than 21,000 individual contractors and subcontractors on the job. Each had to have his own portion of the project completed on schedule and it had to fit perfectly and work exactly as designed.

Although there were many shortcuts, quality and safety were never sacrificed. One of the more dramatic shortcuts demonstrated the inventive spirit of Special Projects. Navy men decided it would take too long to build a submarine from the keel up. Instead, the impatient Polaris men appropriated an attack submarine already well under construction. They split the ship, already approximately 300 feet long, in half, and inserted a 130-foot extra midsection to house the sixteen missiles.

The completed Polaris submarine was as big as an 8,000-ton light cruiser, and as long as one and a half football fields.

Without relying upon visual navigation, this monster of the deep can speed through the undersea darkness at speeds exceeding those of many surface ships and yet navigators know precisely its location at any instant even though they have not seen sun nor stars for weeks at a time. Three independent inertial navigational systems check each other for accuracy. Without any outside information, the "black box" navigation devices record continuously the motion of the ship and the currents of the sea to compute accurately the exact position of the ship. These newly devised electronic navigation systems permit extended cruises under the Arctic ice or anywhere under the sea with absolute safety.

The payload carried in a Polaris submarine's sixteen nuclear-tipped missiles contains a greater explosive punch than was unleashed by all the bombs dropped during World War II. The missile is powered by a two-stage solid fuel rocket motor capable of propelling the warhead some 2,500 miles from submarine to target. Before launching, a battery of fire-control computers feed a constant flow of information into the guidance system. This includes the location of true north, the exact location of the submarine at the moment of firing, the location of the target and the trajectory which must be flown to reach the target from the submarine.

Polaris missiles are launched by air or steam ejection systems which pop them from their submarine launching tubes, forcing them to break the surface of the ocean much like a ping-pong ball will fly into the air if released under water. The instant the base of the missile clears the surface of the sea, the rocket motor ignites to drive the weapon into a ballistic trajectory. The reliability of solid propellants for instantaneous ignition assures accuracy of the missile and increases the safety for submarine and crew against the possibility of the missile falling back into the sea and damaging the submarine. Once launched, the missile is independent of any external commands or controls. An array of gyroscopes, accelerometers, and computers, which comprise the inertial guidance system built into the missile itself, keep it on course, shutting off the rocket motors at the instant required for the missile to fly a natural trajectory to the target.

Endurance is one of the most unique features of Polaris. Cruises normally extend sixty days or more, all of the time spent submerged on station. The *George Washington*, first of the Polaris boats, spent the equivalent of two years under the surface of the sea during the first four years of its operating life. In order to maintain this record, the submarines have the built-in capacity to manufacture their own oxygen from seawater. Special purifying devices remove irritants from the submarines' internal air supplies and maintain the proper balance of oxygen, nitrogen, and other atmospheric elements. Because of the extended cruises and the ability of the ship itself to remain under way month after month with little or no mechanical repair, each Polaris submarine has two crews, a "blue" and a "gold" team, each composed of 140 officers and men. These alternate on two-month patrols. Off-duty crews undergo constant refresher training. Polaris crews are the best-trained sailors in the world. The average precommissioning training period for fleet ballistic missile submariners runs between sixteen and nineteen months. Nine months of this is devoted to formal studies at the United States Guided Missile School at Dam Neck, Virginia. After training in such subjects as transistor theory, digital computer theory, Boolean algebra, and electronics, Polaris men receive additional intensive training in the operations, repair, and maintenance of the equipment and systems found aboard the nuclear submarine.

New advances in very low-frequency radio communications and other types of communications permit the submarines to remain in constant touch with command posts and the rest of the world even though submerged hundreds of feet below the surface of the sea.

Targeting for Polaris submarines is accomplished in the same manner as all other strategic force targeting, by a joint staff under the direction of the nation's Joint Chiefs of Staff. Thus, all strategic deterrent forces—manned aircraft of the Air Force and the Navy and the intermediate and intercontinental ballistic missiles of these two services—are coordinated at all times. In the United States stable of nuclear weapons, Polaris is the one most able to survive initial attacks and is the most dependable under any circumstances.

This nuclear explosive power is carried in a ship which is hard to find and even more difficult to destroy. Polaris is the nearest thing to an invulnerable weapon devised by mankind. This invulnerability of Polaris offers this nation a strategic bonus of time—time for political evaluation, consultation, and action in times of crisis without ever sacrificing the ability to retaliate. In this manner, Polaris submarines now on station in the Atlantic and Pacific oceans decrease greatly the possibility of mutual destruction of the world through a nuclear accident.

The ability of Polaris to prowl the oceans of the world without interference, plus the 2,500-mile range of its missiles, bring all of the world under the direct influence of sea power for the first time in history. This force of forty-one United States Polaris submarines mounting 656 modern nuclear-tipped missiles is the world's most powerful deterrent force for peace. It is a great stabilizer in world affairs. And yet, this is not a force which would attract nuclear bombs to populated areas of the world in an effort to wipe it out should war come. This is a force which moves the nation's nuclear strength away from our cities, away from our shores and into the seas. This is a force which, in peacetime, does not create a demand for expensive real estate of our own or of our allies, thereby creating problems of sovereignty. The seas are free.

Polaris admittedly is an expensive weapon. Although the submarine program is a solid investment in security, planners seek ways of expanding the number of reliable Polaris missiles on station beyond the basic submarine program.

Continued emphasis on the advantages of a sea-based system has caused consideration of surface ships as mobile "silos" for Polaris missiles. Mounted in surface ships, Polaris missiles would add valuable variety to the Western arsenal, complicating the problems of our opponents. A comprehensive study of the vulnerability of the surface Polaris system concluded that the force would survive and an efficient and effective operation would be guaranteed. Merchant hulls would be indistinguishable from thousands of other ships cruising the world's sea-lanes of commerce. They would, in peacetime, be lost in the millions of square miles of ocean space. Surface ships are easy and economical to build and to operate.

In seeking to preserve its freedom, the United States faces the military responsibility of maintaining a strong deterrent force to counter any nuclear blackmail, and at the same time providing the flexibility required to meet military adventures of conventional, non-nuclear nature.

The Navy has always had a major role in meeting conventional threats, and in the second half of the twentieth century the Navy has been given a major deterrent responsibility with the development of the Polaris submarine system, the ultimate in deterrent strength. In turning to a surface ship Polaris force, the United States may well find a way of expanding its deterrent strength and at the same time greatly reducing its cost in dollars, manpower, and real estate, moving its missile bases away from centers of humanity.

⚓

CHAPTER TWELVE

The Navy Service Forces

Due to the vastness of ocean area, World War II in the Pacific presented a gigantic fleet logistic problem which intensified as the Japanese were pushed westward. In order to get maximum combat effectiveness from its fighting ships, the U.S. Navy had to institute all manner of services, including underway replenishment.

Before Pearl Harbor, fueling had been established at sea as standard procedure. Yet very little had been accomplished in the way of actual transfer of provisions, ammunition, and supply from and to ships under way. Soon after Pearl Harbor, on March 1, 1942, the Base Force in the Pacific under Rear Admiral W. L. Calhoun was renamed the Service Force. Eventually Calhoun became a vice admiral and continued to head the Service Force until practically the end of the war. The overall aid rendered to combative types of ships grew into a tremendous endeavor. Early heavy losses in the Asiatic and in the South Pacific areas increased the difficulty of carrying out such operations. Admiral Halsey appointed Captain Worrall R. Carter as Commander, Service Squadron South Pacific, who became a pioneer in service to the combatant units of the fleet. With the beginning of the westward trek in the central Pacific under Admiral Spruance, Captain Carter moved there in the fall of 1943 to lend his superior talents to the Fifth Fleet. He organized the Mobile Service Squadrons, which followed the fleet west in its island-hopping campaign, and established the first base at Majuro, the first of the larger atolls to be so established as a fleet anchorage. He then moved his operation from one successive location to another. Next was Kwajalein, then Eniwetok, followed by Guam and Ulithi.

Then came Leyte, and Samar in the Philippines, and finally several islands in the Ryukyus, including Okinawa. Under Vice Admiral Donald B. Beary, the afloat services that were rendered to ships under way had progressed to the point where the combatant ships could and did get everything they needed by withdrawing during the night to a safe area for a day, then returning to the combat area the next day. Thus, ships could remain on station for indefinite periods without returning to port. Rear Admiral Frederick C. Sherman's task carrier group actually remained at sea for a record of 87 days. This was truly "The Fleet That Came to Stay."

In commenting on this achievement, Fleet Admiral Chester W. Nimitz described the Navy's Service Force as being "our greatest secret weapon of World War II."

During the course of the Korean War, the Pacific Service Force performed excellent assistance to the fighting ships on station in the Sea of Japan and the Yellow Sea to the west of the Korean peninsula. It was comparable to a mobile seagoing service station, available night or day wherever and whenever needed. Included in the Service Force operations are such multitudinous activities as the following:

- Underway replenishment of fuel supplies, ammunition, and certain kinds of repairs.
- Salvage of ships aground.
- Treatment of wounded on hospital ships.
- Hydrographic surveys and "on-the-scene" manufacture of charts for captured harbors.
- Anti-surveillance operations by fleet tugs.
- Support of amphibious operations, where parts have not been developed.
- Development of bases and beachheads in first assault operations, often far from the sea.
- Construction of airfields and port facilities by the Seabees ("CB's" or construction battalions).

In the Vietnam War, the Service Force under Rear Admiral E. B. Hooper has performed in a superior manner by rendering needed

116

services everywhere. Many logistical records of this kind have been established. One such noteworthy accomplishment was by the USS *Katmai* which transferred 813,000 pounds of ammunition to an aircraft carrier in the incredibly swift interval of 56 minutes. A provision ship delivered 755 tons of perishables in only a week's time. Ships on "Yankee Station" off the mainland of Vietnam, the carrier-operating base encompassing a 150-mile radius in the South China Sea, receive sufficient replenishment (often on a day-to-day basis) to enable them to continue operating for three months at a time.

Admiral Hooper, in the Vietnam War, characterizes the efforts of his Service Force as follows: "Regardless of all the technological advances, man remains the key ingredient of naval warfare. Men of the Service Force perform unglamorous jobs involving strenuous effort and long hours—yet their spirit is amazing. They have met every challenge with magnificent performances."

A good example of the floor space alone required for just one day's supplies to support the war in Vietnam would cover a large football field to a depth of thirty feet. In addition, over 5 billion gallons of fuel oil are delivered to the ships involved each month. An aircraft carrier, for example, may use 200,000 gallons of jet airplane fuel in a single day.

The helicopter has proved to be a valuable asset in delivering goods to ships as well as shore-based operations. In some cases, helicopters have ferried needed supplies or parts to ships at a distance of 75 miles away. Many personal transfers are also accomplished by helicopter.

Several new types of ships have been added to the Service Force in order to facilitate service to the fighting fleets. These include container ships, roll-on and roll-off ships, and economical barge carrier systems, such as the Lykes intermodal carrier, which greatly facilitate cargo handling.

The unglamorous side of any naval effort is logistics. Men of the Service Forces, who work long hours under adverse conditions to accomplish logistical supply, are deserving of the highest praise.

Neither the Sixth Fleet in the Mediterranean nor the Seventh Fleet in the Far East could operate without the Service Forces. Indeed, no overseas campaign could be undertaken without the kind of logistics furnished by the Navy's Service Forces.

⚓

CHAPTER THIRTEEN

Military Sea Transportation Service

Closely parallel to the Service Force, but distinctly separate from it, is the Military Sea Transportation Service. As an outgrowth of the Unification Act, the ships of the Army Transport Service Force were combined with Navy transports to form this service. The mission of this agency is to haul troops and freight overseas on a point-to-point basis, rather than provide direct service to ships at sea.

Secretary of Defense Louis Johnson established the Military Sea Transportation Service on October 1, 1949, in accordance with the National Security Act of 1947. Specifically, this organization provides sea transportation for personnel and cargoes of the Department of Defense. It also plans and negotiates for the use of commercial shipping, including, in some cases, foreign flagships to augment its own fleet as necessary to meet total requirements. In addition, it has to plan for, and be capable of, expansion in time of war.

Although operated under the Navy, the Service has broad powers to procure the additional shipping for all branches of the government if so ordered by the Secretary of Defense.

Except for chartered ships, the merchant shipping of this service is ordinarily manned by former merchant marine seamen who now have civil service status. In some cases, Naval personnel may either be assigned in detachments or the entire crew may be Navy men.

The Military Sea Transportation Service conducts its operations to a large extent along commercial lines, transacting much of its business by competitive bidding. Its operations are scrutinized by the Bureau of the Budget, and the number and composition of its fleet are determined by the Joint Chiefs of Staff and the Chief of Naval Operations.

Today, 98 per cent of the cargoes that are delivered to Southeast Asia in support of our economic and military efforts go there by ships, and the great bulk of this is hauled by the Military Sea Transportation Service in U.S. flag merchant marine ships.

The Service has performed many and varied tasks in the past and it will continue to do so in the future. In order to grasp the broad scale of its operations, let us look at the following highlights of the agency's growth and expansion during its first decade.

• In June, 1951, the first Arctic operations began with the Service carrying men and supplies to the Air Force base at Thule, Greenland.

• In 1954, the Service's chartered ships participated in the lifting of 14,500 nonrepatriated Chinese prisoners of war from Korea to Formosa; and, in that same year, thousands of Vietnamese people were evacuated from North Vietnam to escape Communist rule.

Later that year, its ships successfully surveyed and charted a safe passage for deep-draft ships across the top of North America— the Northwest Passage. Persistence, patience, and daring in a decade of Arctic sea lift by this agency's military and civilian crews chartered a deepwater route across the northern seas for commercial shipping in support of the Dew Line. In 1959, the Service commenced a special projects program under which it operated a host of uniquely equipped ships for other agencies of government, such as the Naval Laboratory, Pacific Missile Range, National Aeronautics and Space Administration, and the Air Force.

In 1960, the USNS *Longview*'s helicopters snatched from the Pacific the nose cone of *Discoverer XIII* satellite. This was the first time in history that a man-made object had been recovered from outer space. In 1964 the service transported across the Atlantic Ocean the largest amphibious landing force ever assembled in peacetime. The training exercise, Operation Steelpike, utilized Navy-owned transports and chartered privately owned merchantmen to carry Marines across the seas and deliver them on the beachheads of Spain. In that same year, Fidel Castro turned off the water serving Guantanamo Naval Base. Tankers of this service carried 282,000,000 gallons of water from Florida to Cuba for the American base, providing the sole source of water during the interim before a desalting plant could be installed. The USNS *Corpus Christi*, a former Navy seaplane tender, had been converted by the Service into a floating helicopter maintenance and repair facility for the Army. Sailed by U.S. Merchant Marine personnel having civil service status, the ship carries an Army battalion of approximately 300 mechanics and technicians who service Army's helicopters in harbors of Vietnam. So successful is the operation that the Army is seeking additional floating bases for this purpose. Civilian-chartered ships and military vessels of the Military Sea Transportation Service became important instruments for the continuing battle against the drain of our gold reserves caused by an unfavorable balance of payments. With American forces in Europe consuming 1,500,000 tons of coal and coke each year, "Buy American" restrictions were imposed upon the military. The service was called upon to "deliver the goods." At the peak of the operation, one of its chartered merchant ships carrying 20,000 tons of coal and coke left an American port for Europe every three days. American purchases of beef to feed American troops in Europe were also delivered to destination. Conventional stowage would not meet the demands of American forces in Europe who were consuming 900,000 pounds of beef weekly. The Service and commercial operators combined to develop new stowage methods to meet the needs.

As the scope of the Military Sea Transportation Service operations broadened and its responsibilities increased, this service accepted more and more tasks which required a unique fleet of ships designed for a great variety of specific purposes.

Among these special projects ships operated by the Service are the USNS *Gibbs*, a converted seaplane tender now carrying Columbia University scientists on oceanographic missions; the USNS *Range Recoverer*, equipped with the latest telemetry, data processing and radio instrumentation, and missile recovery equipment for missile experimentation at the NASA operation at Wallops Island, Virginia; USNS *Kingsport*, operating under its command for NASA as a satellite communications ship, which incidentally had a major role in the live television transmission in the United States of the Tokyo Olympic Games; USNS *Gillis*, built from the keel up as a modern oceanographic research ship; and USNS *General Vandenberg*, a C4 converted transport which now tracks missiles and spacecraft for the Air Force and NASA with the world's most sophisticated array of seagoing electronics gear. Others include, USNS *Eltanin*, an ice-resistant cargo ship converted into a seagoing Antarctic scientific research laboratory sponsored by the National Science Foundation; USNS *Bowditch*, designed to survey coastal and oceanic areas of the world; and the USNS *Mission Capistrano*, formerly a tanker and now a research ship carrying the largest oceangoing array of under-water acoustic equipment, which has a well in the center through which can be lowered 350 tons of equipment to reach down 600 feet into the sea.

Thus, in addition to its worldwide responsibilities for ocean transportation in all branches of the Department of Defense, MSTS is serving other agencies who are turning more and more to the oceans of the world for research, communication, food, and other natural resources. While meeting these diverse and widespread missions, the agency has proved by its excellent response during the international crises in Korea, Vietnam, and elsewhere in the world that it can perform its first and basic mission in immediate sea-lift capability in times of emergency. Today Military Sea Trans-portation Service owned ships and privately owned American flag vessels under charter to the MSTS are carrying virtually all of the cargo going overseas to United States military forces throughout the world. Less than two per cent of the supplies shipped to our troops overseas in Asia or in Europe are airlifted. As Vice Admiral Glynn R. Donaho, Commander of the Military Sea Transportation Service, has written in *Navy*, "The Magazine of Seapower,"—"The broad scope of these naval and shipping operations requires MSTS at all times to be responsive to changes in international, diplomatic, com-mercial and monetary affairs, customs requirements, and port fa-cilities; far-flung military operations—actual and anticipated; global weather and sea conditions; domestic and foreign labor union and commercial shipping practices, ad infinitum."

The success of this effort can best be shown by the magnitude of the worldwide operation which the Military Sea Transportation Service has recently conducted. First, the movement of as many as 425,000 passengers in a single year. And, second, the transportation of 24 million tons of dry cargo and 60 billion gallons of petroleum products in a 12-month period.

Vice Admiral Lawson P. Ramage, Commander of the Military Sea Transportation Service, has stated: "To truly deliver the goods wherever the American fighting man is called upon to serve in the defense of security and freedom has become the responsibility of the U.S. Navy and Merchant Marine. This is accomplished by the Navy's Service Forces in the Atlantic and Pacific Fleets and by the Military Sea Transportation Service, augmented as necessary by various types of ships from the American Merchant Marine."

123

⚓

CHAPTER FOURTEEN

The United States Merchant Marine

In times of peace, the United States Merchant Marine has found itself in a position not unlike that of Kipling's Tommy Atkins. When an emergency situation arises, the United States will build much-needed ships on an all-out basis. But too quickly, when the crisis ends, we forget that our nation's Merchant Marine is "Our Fourth Arm of National Defense." Indeed, it is necessary to our national welfare in peace that this arm be ready for possible military service in national emergency.

The U.S. government tried to compensate for this false economy of peacetime valleys and wartime peaks by passing the Merchant Marine Act of 1936. But this act was never implemented. After World War II, the United States had literally thousands of modern ships. Now, however, in the short span of two decades, we have fallen from the leading maritime nation to the position of fourteenth in commercial ship tonnage.

One of the great handicaps to the United States Merchant Marine is the high cost of American labor as compared to foreign labor. It is difficult, if not impossible, for U.S. shipowners to compete in the world market without government subsidy. Many ship operators have resorted to foreign flags, or "flags of convenience," and man their ships with foreign seamen in order to use cheap labor.

The best way to meet such competition is to build larger, faster, automated ships. The larger ship can naturally haul more cargo. The faster ship requires less voyage time, and the automated ship can be operated with fewer crewmen. If nuclear-powered ships were built in large numbers, the cost of power plants could be reduced to acceptable levels. In addition, they could be operated at high speeds with minimal repairs. A properly automated ship could be operated with a crew of a dozen men. The tonnage of ships has so increased that 300,000-ton tankers are now being built, with 500,000-ton ships in the planning stage.

Meanwhile, the Communist countries of the world have recognized the need to maintain a strong merchant marine. For example, the Soviet Union has embarked on a shipbuilding program which calls for a twelve-to-one ratio, as compared to our new-ship construction. By 1980, if this schedule is maintained, the Soviets' tonnage of commercial ships will be twice that of the United States. Our budget calls for 13 merchant ships to be constructed in 1968; in the same year, the USSR will overtake the United States in total overall commercial capability. In 1966, Soviet ships outnumbered United States ships. The Soviets have 585 ships of more than 1,000 tons each in their merchant fleet.

At present, greater emphasis is placed by the Soviets on dry-cargo ships, because of the greater need for them, but tankers, passenger ships, and specialized-type vessels are being built in appreciable numbers.

The influence of the Soviet Union on world affairs is bound to increase in direct proportion to the growth of Soviet sea power. In the early 1930's, Stalin recognized the importance of merchant-ship power. At that time, he laid the plans which today are making the USSR a strong maritime nation. In many categories, the types of ships being built by the Soviets are ultramodern. East Germany, Bulgaria, and Yugoslavia have excellent shipyards but the Soviet Union purchases many of its ships from free countries such as England, Japan, Finland, Sweden, and Italy.

Already the Soviet Union has been able to manipulate ocean freight rates to undercut free-world prices for hauling cargo. Recently it has sold oil up to 20 per cent cheaper than the going world prices. The Soviets have also opened a northern shipping lane through the ice from the Atlantic to the Pacific by use of a nuclear-powered icebreaker, making it available to all on a toll basis.

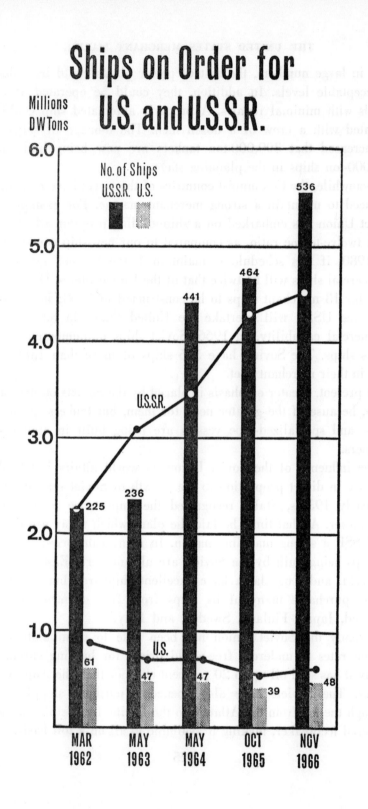

Ships on Order for U.S. and U.S.S.R.

Millions
DW Tons

No. of Ships
U.S.S.R.   U.S.

6.0

5.0

4.0

3.0

U.S.S.R.

2.0

1.0

U.S.

| MAR 1962 | MAY 1963 | MAY 1964 | OCT 1965 | NOV 1966 |

225   236   441   464   536

61   47   47   39   48

If the United States does not take prompt and drastic action to meet this challenge, the day may soon come when Soviet shipping may be an even greater factor in aiding the Communists to achieve their stated goal of world domination. It could be an even greater aid than all their war-making materials combined, including missiles. As their merchant sea power increases, their acts of aggression may be expected to occur more frequently in the trouble spots of the world. The United States would then be called upon to fight an increasing number of limited wars, if we hope to survive in a free world.

When Admiral Mahan said that a navy *plus* bases *plus* a merchant marine *equals* sea power, he was defining a geopolitical equation which, with minor modifications, is equally valid in today's space age. Ironically, Mahan wanted a navy to protect the trade routes. Now the Navy is an instrument of national policy and we are using our Merchant Marine to support all the armed services in carrying our overseas commitments. Two-thirds of the men and 98 per cent of the cargoes which the United States needs to support a sustained overseas military operation are transported by a combination of U.S. Navy and Merchant Marine ships—chiefly the latter. Although both of the moving elements of Mahan's equation are composed of seagoing ships, any comparison of the U.S. Navy with the Merchant Marine offers a distinct contrast. The Navy is an organization under the Executive branch of our government, established and regulated by law, whereas Merchant Marine ships are privately owned.

There can be no single, simple definition of the Merchant Marine to which all concerned will agree. This agency includes noncombatant ships of the nation, both privately and publicly owned, and the personnel necessary to man them. Naturally, since industry is an important adjunct of national policy, the shipping companies must remain prosperous and healthy. Included in the maritime industry are not only the shipping companies that operate passenger cargo and tanker types of carriers, but the shipyards as well.

The Federal Maritime Commission today is a five-man regulatory board, of which Rear Admiral John Harlee is chairman. It functions under the President to establish the rates, services, and practices necessary to keep the U.S. Merchant Marine in a healthy state.

The Maritime Administration, now headed by Acting Administrator J. W. Gulick, is charged with fostering the development and encouraging the maintenance of the U.S. Merchant Marine. It operates under the Department of Commerce and may soon be transferred to the new Department of Transportation. It provides subsidies needed to adjust the difference in building and operating costs, including wage costs for keeping the U.S. shipping companies in operation. It also pays for any national defense features added to the ships. In addition, it approves the transfer of ships to foreign flag or registry.

The agency also operates and maintains the United States Merchant Marine Academy at Kings Point, New York, to provide the academic background and the nautical education essential to a successful career at sea. Midshipmen are nominated by their Senators and Representatives and appointed by the Maritime Administrator to the Academy for education and training to fit them to become officers in the United States Merchant Marine. After successful completion of the four-year course of study, graduates receive a Merchant Marine Officer's license, and are commissioned Ensigns in the United States Naval Reserve; in addition they receive the degree of Bachelor of Science.

The United States offers to qualified young men interested in a career at sea an opportunity to attend the United States Merchant Marine Academy. Under the able direction of Rear Admiral Gordon McLintock, superintendent for the past twenty years, many young men have benefited by this opportunity and have outstanding careers in the Merchant Marine and the U.S. Navy.

The Maritime Administration supervises government grants and student aid to state maritime academies. The states of New York, California, Maine, Massachusetts, and Texas have these state maritime academies. The agency also participates in port promotional activities and international matters relating to general ship operations. Further, it is charged with research and development affecting the shipping industry—having built the nuclear ship, **the** NS

Savannah, the world's first nuclear-powered merchant ship, and the SS *Denison*, the first U.S. oceangoing hydrofoil.

The NS *Savannah*, which originally operated regularly and successfully as a nuclear "atoms for peace" demonstration vessel—having made prominent visits to many maritime powers—was later converted to freight-ship duties which she is carrying out at present. While the *Savannah* was not designed as a profit-making vessel, she is doing very creditably carrying commercial cargo. The ship also serves as a valuable basis for the future enlargement of the Nuclear Merchant Marine. Based on the NS *Savannah*'s experience in engineering, training, and personnel management, many ways have been developed to improve the second-generation nuclear merchant ships. The ship regularly carries Merchant Marine Academy midshipmen, and a training officer who supervises them. An extensive study is now being conducted for the account of the Maritime Administration Office of Research and Development to enable it to actually lay out the physical design and power plant of the next large nuclear merchant ships.

Since the birth of our nation, the U.S. Merchant Marine has played an important role in the growth of the country and, in wartime, this has meant the difference between victory and defeat.

In World War I, the United States built, on a crash program, some 2,316 ships totaling 14,000,000 tons at a cost of some 3 billion dollars. After the war, this fleet was allowed to dwindle to insignificance.

In 1936, an effort was made to bolster up our merchant marine in an attempt to prepare for impending war. Thus, at least a foundation was laid to meet the expansion brought on by the war when it actually came. Under the supervision of Vice Admiral Emory S. Land, the merchant fleet construction of World War II was on the order of some 5,000 ships, totaling 54,000,000 tons.

The sea-lift operations carried out during World War II were staggering. Some 268,000,000 tons of supplies and equipment were moved by the U.S. Merchant Marine fleet. In addition, some 7,100,-000 troops and 141,000 civilians were carried overseas.

The cost of this lift was high. More than 600 ships were sunk and

6,249 merchant seamen lost their lives, a figure which includes 210 U.S. Merchant Marine Academy midshipmen. German submarines operating in the Atlantic were responsible for most of this toll. Until the United States could develop hunter-killer groups to stop them, these submarines were sinking our ships at an appalling rate. One convoy, *PQ-17*, on the run to Murmansk during July, 1942, had 22 ships out of 50 sunk, with nearly all the rest suffering damages.

In September, 1942, the SS *Stephen Hopkins*, a Liberty ship, was attacked by the German auxiliary cruiser *Stier*, aided by her supply ship *Tannenfels*. With a single 5-inch gun, *Stephen Hopkins* retaliated by sinking the *Stier*, but at the same time was herself in a sinking condition. Thirty-one of her crew, including the captain, perished. The remaining crew finally abandoned ship. One member, however, nineteen-year-old Midshipman-Engineer Edwin J. O'Hara, on seeing *Tannenfels* move in to pick up German survivors, manned the gun and fired five rounds at close range into the German ship before his ship carried him down with it. Meantime, survivors of the *Stephen Hopkins* undertook to sail in the lifeboat to the coast of Brazil—a distance of 1,500 miles. Three of their number died enroute, but the rest made it. The heroics of the *Stephen Hopkins* crew are difficult to surpass in the annals of the sea.

The record of the U.S. Merchant Marine in World War II is a credit to the nation and their deeds were an important contribution to eventual victory. Since World War II, there has been, by actual count no fewer than forty shooting wars. A list of the most important includes those in Korea, Kashmir, Greece, Israel, Malaya, Hungary, Cyprus, Goa, the Congo, Venezuela, the Dominican Republic, and Vietnam. During the Korean War alone, 73,000,000 tons of cargo and 5,000,000 passengers were moved by ships, 84 per cent of which were merchant vessels. Korea again demonstrated the need for a strong U.S. Merchant Marine fleet. Now we have a comparable situation all over again in Vietnam.

To remedy this obvious maritime gap, 172 ships to date have been removed from the mothball reserve at a cost of $500,000 each. The United States shipping lines have responded to the call of duty in a highly creditable manner, but in order to do so have had to give up

American flag-line trade—in the amount of $16,500,000—to ships of other nations. It will be difficult to recapture this substantial trade once taken over by foreign ships.

It is now apparent to the entire world that the United States has now reached the point of being dependent on the ships of other nations for products without which our economy would disintegrate and our military potential fade away. American flagships are carrying less than 10 per cent of the tonnage that enters our ports each year. The foreign-owned ships naturally are available to us only at the will of their home countries.

In peacetime we must prepare for war and build up the U.S. Merchant Marine to such a degree that it can assume its proper position of emergency effort. If the U.S. Merchant Marine is to be saved like the Ancient Mariner from "the fiends that plague him thus," a direct and positive course of action must be set. The merchant marine industry, which means labor, shipowners, and shipbuilders, must realize the importance of a strong merchant marine to our great maritime nation. Recently there have been efforts on the part of labor leaders to effect measures to improve the U.S. Merchant Marine but the parties involved will have to accept practical solutions. Congress will have to provide subsidies as necessary or tax reductions which will enable the shipowners to survive. The public must be properly informed to make it realize that adequate building of modern ships for the U.S. Merchant Marine is a necessity in order to provide security in both peace and war. The fundamental problem is not one of governmental support necessary to an industry; it is the problem of its own needs supported by the maritime industry. It is cooperation by all the facets of the industry that will revitalize our merchant marine.

⚓

CHAPTER FIFTEEN

The United States Coast Guard

In order to insure that revenues were collected, Alexander Hamilton, Secretary of the Treasury, persuaded Congress to establish a fleet of ten armed boats—36 to 40 feet in length—in 1790. This service was called the Revenue Marine, but in time the designation was changed to the Revenue Cutter Service. The first of these boats was the *Massachusetts*, a two-masted schooner of about 70 tons, a fast sailer, mounting six swivel guns.

In 1799, the revenue cutters were ordered to operate under the Secretary of the Navy in the quasi-war against France. This principle has been followed since those early days in the history of the United States. During every war since the Revolution, Coast Guardsmen have fought alongside Navy men. Individual acts of heroism by men of this service were numerous. They took a double oath, to support the Constitution and to prevent frauds against revenue. During the war with France, in 1799, the cutter *Eagle*, a 187-ton vessel, captured five French ships, retook seven American vessels, and helped in capturing ten others.

In 1812, with the war still in its first few days, the cutter *Jefferson* captured the British *Patriot*. The small cutters of that day frequently met and defeated larger, more heavily armed British men-of-war.

The first record of the Coast Guard on a search and rescue mission is in an 1831 order issued by the Secretary of the Treasury Louis McLane, directing revenue cutters to winter patrols on designated stations. Men of the Revenue Cutter Service were, by this time,

132

enforcing laws concerning piracy, plundering, quarantine, slave trade, and navigation.

By the start of the Civil War, the Coast Guard's predecessor had built the cutter *Harriet Lane,* a side-wheel wooden steam cutter. She was assigned to a naval force relieving Fort Sumter. It was during this action that she fired the first naval shot of the Civil War. Another cutter, the *Naugatuck,* was escort vessel for the *Monitor* when she steamed into Hampton Roads to engage with the *Merrimac* in that famous naval battle of ironclads.

The Spanish-American War again found cutters fighting alongside the ships of the Navy: the *McCulloch* with Dewey in the Philippines; *Windom* and *Hudson* in Cuba; and fifteen others elsewhere.

During the period from just before the Spanish-American War until 1915, the service saw many changes. The Revenue Cutter Service and Life Saving Service were merged, and the name "Coast Guard" was born. It was during this time that aviation was adopted by the Coast Guard. In 1916 a flying surfboat was ordered for the Coast Guard. This seaplane was the forerunner of the Navy's *NC-4,* which was the first to fly across the Atlantic in 1919. Lieutenant Commander A. C. Read, U.S. Navy, was the pilot and Lieutenant Elmer F. Stone, U.S. Coast Guard, was copilot.

Again, at the outbreak of World War I, the ships and 2,500 men of the Coast Guard were ordered to duty under the Navy; Coast Guardsmen and their ships were assigned primarily to antisubmarine and convoy escort duties. It is of some interest to note that a larger relative percentage of Coast Guardsmen than any other branch of the armed forces were killed in action during this war. Men of this service were often engaged in action on the high seas.

After World War I, the Coast Guard resumed its peacetime role. Early in 1920, Congress enacted the Prohibition Act. Not only did illicit stills and the product "moonshine" multiply, but great quantities of alcoholic liquor were smuggled across the oceans and over the borders of the United States. Smuggling by sea was less subject to hijackers or law enforcement interceptions. With the long U.S. coastlines, and thousands of bays and inlets, it was relatively easy

133

for small speedy craft, under the cover of darkness or fog, to bring thousands of cases of foreign liquor from larger ships which were lying outside of the twelve-mile limit and which were thus safe from interference. The Secretary of the Treasury ordered the Coast Guard to prevent such favored methods of bringing illegal liquor into the country.

Since smuggling was not confined to one area, it took a great number of ships and boats, men, and a great deal of money to enforce what later proved to be an unpopular and almost unenforceable law.

Coast Guard forces in the Atlantic, Pacific, and Gulf Coasts, and on the Great Lakes were increased. In order to capture these rum-runners, the Coast Guard borrowed the technique of some of the rumrunner boats to construct high-powered speedboats with very stout hulls which could withstand heavy seas. This type led to the development of high-speed crash and rescue vessels. Later the stout-hull principle was adopted as a prototype for the torpedo boats of World War II.

Two separate actions by President Franklin D. Roosevelt in 1939 had a great effect on the future of the Coast Guard. When the war broke out in Europe in September, Coast Guard units were ordered to carry out extensive patrols to insure that merchant ships in U.S. waters did not violate the neutrality of the United States. This was followed by port security operations established in the Espionage Act of 1917 and the Dangerous Cargo Act. The other unrelated action by the President was the transfer of the Bureau of Lighthouses to the Department of the Treasury for consolidation within the Coast Guard. This brought together two government functions primarily concerned with safety of mariners. Two years later the maritime safety package was completed with the addition of the Bureau of Marine Inspection and Navigation. Now virtually all matters dealing with safety at sea were under one agency—the Coast Guard.

World War II brought to the service an expansion never dreamed of before. Personnel wearing the shield of the Coast Guard were in many fields of naval operations. They were on antisubmarine duty; they escorted convoys; they were in search and rescue units wherever the United States had forces; they guarded U.S. ports; they walked the beaches on guard against infiltrating agents; they were coxswains of assault boats in major amphibious landings; they provided a special patrol in the English Channel during the Normandy invasion where they were credited with saving thousands of lives; they manned both attack and troop transports. World War II once again demonstrated the versatility of the Coast Guard.

Along with the electronic development of radar and sonar came loran (*long-range aid to navigation*). Although developed as a wartime instrument to assist navigators in locating their positions, it was so well received by all who use the air and sea that it was retained after the war and is still being operated and further developed by the Coast Guard.

Demobilization after the war cut deeply into the muscle of the Coast Guard. Ships were tied up for lack of crews, and shore stations were far below the minimum manning standards necessary to accomplish operational missions.

A postwar study done by a commercial management consultant for both Congress and the Treasury Department brought out what was already known within the service. More personnel and funds were needed to accomplish the tasks assigned to the Coast Guard. This was the start needed to help the service on an uphill climb to the plateau of stability it needed.

The limited war in Korea imposed special requirements on the Coast Guard. Ships were rearmed for possible action. The partially dormant port security program was revitalized. New loran stations were constructed to provide navigational aids for aircraft and ships operating in an area where there were few aids. Search and Rescue units were established throughout the Pacific. Additional ocean stations were established in the western Pacific to provide weather data and additional rescue facilities. Some activities were discontinued after the war, but others, such as the loran stations were made permanent and were expanded.

Since the Korean War the Coast Guard has grown by leaps and bounds. New aircraft and ships have been provided to modernize the service. Helicopters have been added for air-sea rescue.

From the original relatively simple task of collecting customs in the 1790's the roles and missions of the Coast Guard have multiplied and expanded. Search and Rescue has now become a complex air-sea science. Many aids to navigation have been placed in U.S. harbors, lakes, and rivers and oceans as well. On-scene search and rescue facilities have been established at island stations in both the Atlantic and Pacific oceans. The United States merchant fleet today is afforded the best safety facilities in the world. Marine law enforcement in the field of recreational boating is an important function of the Coast Guard. Oceanography, meteorology, and ice breaking are performed when practicable by the Coast Guard not only in the Arctic and Antarctic oceans but in U.S. inland waters, such as the Great Lakes. Military preparedness to enable the Coast Guardsmen to play their part alongside Defense Department personnel is a prime requisite of the Coast Guard. Great emphasis is placed on reserve training by the Coast Guard in order to meet wartime expansion needs.

In April, 1967, with the creation of the Department of Transportation, the Coast Guard moved out of the Treasury Department. The Coast Guard joined the Federal Aviation Administration, the Federal Highway Administration, the Federal Railroad Administration, and the St. Lawrence Seaway Corporation in forming a new federal Department of Transportation. Under this new department, the Coast Guard has acquired added new responsibilities, some transferred from the Bureau of Customs and others from the U.S. Army Corps of Engineers. Its relationship to the other services remains unchanged. Under law, in case of war, the Coast Guard is automatically assigned to the Navy. Also at other times, if needed, the President may assign the Coast Guard to the Navy. In the case of Vietnam, by agreement between the Commandant of the Coast Guard and the Chief of Naval Operations, Coast Guard units in the area now operate under the Navy.

Coast Guard Squadrons One and Three are under Navy Operational Control. Squadron One, made up of twenty-six 82-foot patrol boats, and Squadron Three, composed of five major cutters, are major forces in "Market Time," a designation given to the blockade operation denying access to enemy forces trying to infiltrate South

Vietnam by sea. Coast Guardsmen have captured many enemy boats carrying tons of weapons together with many suspected Vietcong. In addition they have provided fire support to ground troops during many missions in Southeast Asia.

Referring to the future of his service, Admiral Willard J. Smith, Commandant of the Coast Guard, has stated, "the Coast Guard is ready, able, and willing to discharge its obligations and responsibilities as an integral part of our nation's sea power."

⚓

CHAPTER SIXTEEN

Secrets of the Sea

In August, 1962, *Mariner II* was launched from Cape Kennedy. Days later from 54 million miles in space, the spacecraft reported that the temperature on Venus was 800 degrees. The satellite then proceeded on to orbit the sun. This was a spectacular scientific achievement and the knowledge acquired was necessary in the exploration of space.

In April, 1963, eight months later, the nuclear attack submarine *Thresher* made a routine test dive east of Cape Cod. After a garbled message, the *Thresher* was not heard from again. Not until months later did the deep-sea research vehicle *Trieste* manage to locate and recover broken bits and pieces of the submarine.

Ironically, we could man space vehicles sailing hundreds of miles in the sky and could track satellites through millions of miles of space, but we could not peer through slightly more than a mile and a half of water which covers three fourths of our earth's surface. Today, we know more about the surface of the moon than we do about the bottom of the sea.

The ability to completely understand the ocean, to predict its behavior, and to use its potential in peace and war are essential to American security and progress. The key to achieving this understanding is found in a relatively new science called oceanography.

Oceanography can be defined as the geography of the ocean and the collective study of all the phenomena of the seas. This all-inclusive science concerns the motions of the seas, the waves, the tides, the currents, and the turbulence of the seas. Marine biology encompasses plants and animals of the sea, ranging from one-cell plankton to whales. Ninety per cent of the world's animal life still lives in the sea.

The science dealing with the ocean floor, its shape, and its multi-billion-year history is submarine geology. The composition of the ocean, the distribution of the elements within it, and the processes which take place in it compose marine chemistry. Since all of these combine to make up the science of oceanography, it can be considered not as one science, but rather the application of all the earth sciences, physical and chemical, biological and geological, to the environment of the seas. It is all-inclusive, extending from the atmosphere which surrounds the world down to the depths of the landmasses lying beneath the oceans. The study of oceanography touches everything between these two extremes, including the interaction of the ocean, the atmosphere, and the sun, which creates the world's weather patterns.

Not until we have obtained a far greater knowledge of the oceans will we be able to take advantage of climate control and all its many benefits, or even improve our weather forecasting. It is estimated that a 50-per-cent improvement in long-range weather forecasting would save the American people 2 billion dollars annually through better storm and drought preparedness, flood control, improved planting and harvesting of crops, more efficient movement and storage of fuels, and wiser planning and timing of road and other major construction projects.

More than one hundred years ago, Navy Lieutenant Matthew Fontaine Maury became the world's first true oceanographer. From his data on ocean currents and winds, he was able to chart the fastest trade routes for clipper-ship captains in one of the most competitive maritime eras of history. Following Maury's example, the British recognized the advantages gained through scientific study of the oceans and undertook the first extensive, worldwide oceanographic survey with the HMS *Challenger* in 1872. Although it has been nearly a century since these first surveys were made, advances in mapping the ocean floor have been slow. Many of the maps and charts which we use today are primitive. Compared to land maps, they are about as accurate as the maps that were used in the year 1700. Only two per cent of the oceans have been charted adequately; only nine per cent of the ocean areas have been explored.

Exploration has been mostly along the continental shelves, first discovered by the British in their early research. These shelves slope gradually from the shoreline at a rate of about 10 feet per mile, before the terrain plunges suddenly downward to the ocean depths, where the average depth exceeds 10,000 feet. The continental shelf off the coasts of California and Chile extends for only a mile or so from the coast. Off northern Europe and Siberia, the shelf reaches some 750 miles into the sea.

Under the deep sea lies a world virtually unknown to man. The terrain is as rough as the Alps. Some peaks exceed the height of Mount Everest. Gorges deeper than the Grand Canyon of the Colorado River have been explored. Great rivers flow about the world's oceans.

Samplings of the ocean bottom one and two miles below the surface indicate that sediment, deposited through the ages, covers the hard crust of the earth. Core samplings in some areas show that it took a thousand years to collect an inch of sediment. In other areas, it is estimated that a thirty-foot core takes history as far back as nine million years. Chemical analysis of the sediment bank may reveal many of history's secrets. In the Pacific, for instance, vast areas of the sea show evidence of a thick layer of ash left in the wake of a massive volcanic eruption which occurred between sixty and eighty thousand years ago.

Above the bottom of the sea, the ocean waters are in constant motion. Currents flow about the world, and flow from the surface to the bottom, carrying life-giving oxygen to life at the bottom of the sea. One current discovered two miles beneath the surface of the Bay of Bengal carries a volume of water estimated at twenty-five times greater than the flow at the mouth of the Mississippi River. In the Pacific, the Humboldt current exerts a direct influence upon the west coast of South America, keeping this region dry and barren. A small shift in the course of this current once a decade has resulted in torrential rains and floods. Should this oceanic river change its course permanently, the whole composition of the region would be dramatically changed. In the Atlantic, the Gulf Stream dominates the weather patterns of many areas. This river, 40 miles wide and 3,000 feet deep, moves northward from the Caribbean at a speed of 50 miles a day. The warm water flows along the east coast of Florida, Georgia, and the Carolinas before it breaks into two branches at Cape Hatteras. The northern stream swings across the North Atlantic and provides an ice-free sea route to Murmansk, north of the Arctic Circle, and other regions of northern Europe. The southern arm flows to the Azores and Africa, swinging south and then west again, completing the general clockwise rotation of water in the Atlantic north of the equator.

In the late 1700's, Benjamin Franklin prepared early maps of a portion of the Gulf Stream and thereby laid the foundation for the concept of thermometrical navigation. He did this by comparing temperatures of water dipped up from the ocean with an old oaken bucket. Modern technology has improved the technique. Today, oceanographers use a shiny metal bucket.

Another moving ocean phenomenon is the *Tusunami*, produced by a sudden, large-scale movement of the ocean floor or seashore, such as a volcanic eruption, earthquake, or landslide. In mid-ocean, wave crests caused by these erratic changes of the contour of the ocean floor may be only a few inches high, but as they speed shoreward at hundreds of miles per hour, coastal shelves build the waves into great walls of water capable of inflicting tremendous destruction of life and property by their incredible force. A small twelve-foot wave just one foot thick packs a hundred-ton wallop. Oceanographic research should make warnings possible in advance for coastal communities in the path of these destructive waves.

Many scientists believe life began in the sea and that it existed there centuries before it developed on land. They strengthen this position with the argument that every major family of life on earth has its more primitive members in the ocean even today. Yet we know surprisingly little about sea life and its habits. Captain Jacques Yves Cousteau, the famous French pioneer bathyscape explorer, reported that some type of animal about the size of a rat moves several inches a second under the layer of sediment covering the bottom of the sea.

141

We have no clue as to what type of animal this is. Nor do we know what causes an entire school of fish to turn suddenly and move out in another direction with the precision of a skilled drill team. Every year thousands of walrus congregate in the Aleutian Islands for mating season. Then they disappear. Where do they go? Wherever it is, sea life must be abundant, for the ocean furnishes their food. The huge California sardine population and the schools of Alaskan salmon have moved to new waters. Where and why we do not know. Man has fought and studied sharks for centuries, but we do not know whether one of the two separate hearing mechanisms which sharks have is truly a "sixth sense." Porpoises, we know, have built-in sonar systems with which they send out sound signals and measure the return echo when searching for food, just like a destroyer hunting unseen submarine targets. We know that the pulse rate is 80 per second for the general search, but lowers to 30 per second when contact is made and the porpoise follows the "beam" to his dinner. How do they do it? We do not know. Dolphins move through the water with ten times more efficiency than torpedoes of the same size and power. Why? Again, we do not know, but when scientists find out, it will revolutionize ship and underwater weapons design.

The potential for biological research in the oceans of the world is virtually unlimited.

Much has been said about the world's population explosion. Every day the number of people in the world is 100,000 more than it was the day before. It has been estimated that as many as seven of every ten men, women, and children in the world will go to bed hungry tonight. There are a billion and a half people alive today who have never had an adequate supply of protein in their diet. In many regions, protein-deficiency diseases are a way of life, in spite of the fact that a pinch or two of powdered, dehydrated, defatted fish meat in the daily diet of a child dying of one such disease, called Kwashiorkor, can revive the child to health in a few days without any additional medication.

It would take only a 30-per-cent increase in the world's fish catch to provide enough protein to eliminate the deficiency, but this will never be achieved as long as man relies on fishing practices which have not changed substantially since ancient times, which is especially true in areas where protein hunger is the greatest. With present fishing practices and yields, the world will be producing less than half the fish protein needed when the new century opens.

The natural resource is present. Oceanographers believe that fishing production can be increased as much as 500 per cent without disturbing the equilibrium of life in the oceans. Dr. W. M. Chapman, president of the Van Camp Foundation, estimates that there is enough protein in the sea to feed 30 billion people adequately if the harvest is made more efficient. Costs must be reduced to the level where the fishing industry can compete profitably with the production of livestock on land.

This opens up the whole new field of "aquaculture"—the production of foodstuffs in the sea instead of in the soil. Imaginative Dr. Athelstan Spilhaus, Dean of the University of Minnesota Institute of Technology, who combines teaching with writing comic strips about the new age in which we live, is among the leading exponents of aquaculture as an independent science. Fish, he believes, can be raised in much the same way that western ranchers raise cattle. Schools of fish may be herded from place to place or fenced in to specific pastures, Dr. Spilhaus believes, if we can learn the secrets of their natural movements. Selective breeding could build bigger and better varieties. Cultivation of fish-grazing areas could improve feeding conditions. If one believes that nothing is impossible, the whole field of fishery management is open. As Dr. Spilhaus says, fishing today is "like a blind man with a butterfly net." The Navy's chief oceanographer, Admiral Denys Knoll, puts it another way when he comments that commercial fishing is carried on with the efficiency of Indians hunting buffalo.

Fish is not the only food to be found in the sea. Vegetation and the minute sea life of the oceans offer a great potential for a multitude of foods, some of which are now being produced in limited quantities. An algae food derivative has been used successfully in bread, noodles, soup, and even ice cream. Marine biologists believe that other tasty fruits and vegetables can be developed by hybridizing the weeds of the sea.

143

Hunger and malnutrition are basic factors in massive social unrest. What man or society will not turn to violence, if necessary, to feed his family? To prevent this in a world rapidly becoming critically overcrowded, man must turn to the nutrient-rich seas for more food. No longer can we deny ourselves the full harvest of the animal and plant kingdom of the seas. No longer can we permit great numbers of fish to die of old age while people die of hunger.

The sea is also a tremendous storehouse for at least fifty minerals, some of which are found in strange places. Cobalt has been extracted from lobsters. Vanadium is in the blood of sea cucumbers. Nickel is found in certain mollusks. Fifty per cent of the world's available oil resources lie under the water in a vast, scarcely touched reserve which has only been scratched by United States coastal operations off the shores of California, Texas, and Louisiana. Exciting quantities of diamonds are being mined from the African continental shelf. Tin is recovered from the ocean floor off Malaysia. Sulfer is pumped from under the sea. Iodine is recovered from Japanese waters and chemical firms extract from seawater all the magnesium and three fourths of all the bromide produced in the United States. Nine thousand feet below the surface of the Pacific, nodules heavy in manganese, iron, and copper have been found. Soon these will be mined, possibly by giant seagoing vacuum sweepers. Potash, needed so desperately as fertilizer for our soils, can be produced from the sea. Skeletons of microscopic sea animals offer the same calcium carbonate composition as land sources of cement. With the present state of technology, it is possible to extract aluminum, lithium, fluorine, iron, and bromine from seawater. Salt, of course, is the natural product of the sea.

Recovery of these minerals as a by-product of desalinization of seawater to provide fresh water for a thirsty world will reduce the cost of domestic and industrial water. In an article prepared for the Navy League's Magazine of Seapower, *Navy*, Robert Abel, executive secretary of the United States Inter-Agency Committee on Oceanography, points out that in the conversion of seawater into seven billion gallons of fresh water, the sludge which is left over will contain the following:

1,000,000 tons of salt
8,000,000 tons of magnesium
2,000,000 tons of potash
  250,000 tons of bromine
   50,000 tons of strontium

Although fiction writers for years have talked about recovery of gold from the sea, this is the least important of the metallic resources of the oceans. Only six pounds of gold would be found in those millions of tons of sludge mentioned above. It would take a cubic mile of seawater to produce thirty-eight pounds of gold, even if we could efficiently extract it from the sea.

Dr. Milner Schaefer, Director of the University of California Institute of Marine Resources, suggests another benefit of seawater conversion, one far more valuable than gold, if nuclear energy is utilized in the process. Excess heat, he proposes, would be generated.

Unlocking this treasure chest of raw materials and putting them to beneficial use is the bread-and-butter challenge which faces ocean-ography in the immediate future. Success will require sizable investments of time, money, and energy, but the return from the harvest of this wealth will be manifold. And it will be just the beginning.

We have hardly scratched the surface of the sea in our research so far. From what we have found it can be assumed that the oceans still hold undreamed-of secrets, virtually unlimited in scope. The nation which becomes a truly knowledgeable sea power through the study of the seas will reap many benefits other than the harvest of foods and minerals which we can predict today. The scientific by-products of this research will open new doors in our oceanic world. Already a broad variety of imaginative concepts are being considered seriously by scientists.

Control of barnacles, for instance, could save the shipping industry hundreds of millions of dollars spent each year in hull maintenance. Barnacles also rob commercial and naval vessels of operating efficiency which can be translated into dollars and cents.

Improved weather forecasting, and ultimately control, will reduce

145

many of the uncertainties of shipping operations and result in speedier deliveries.

More efficient and economical commercial shipping operations can be achieved through better understanding of the movement of wind, waves, and currents. The greatest oceanic tragedy of the twentieth century could have been avoided if, in 1912, navigators had had more precise knowledge of North Atlantic currents, their intensity, their direction and consistency in the springtime, and the movement of icebergs along these currents. The *Titanic*, on her maiden voyage, carried more than twelve hundred men, women, and children to their deaths when she sank after sideswiping an iceberg. Fuller understanding of the movement of ocean waters will not only lead to better selection of oceanic routes, but could also ultimately revolutionize the design of ships.

The dependence of the United States upon oceanic trade will increase by 50 per cent in the next few years. Exports and imports will reach a volume of 400 to 500 million tons annually. With shipping costs averaging twelve dollars per ton, any small reduction in the cost per ton of moving this cargo, will multiply into millions of dollars every year. Oceanographers can help reduce these costs and make America's merchant marine more competitive through more efficient forecasting of currents, waves, and winds; through discovery and use of oceanic "jetstreams" similar to those high-altitude winds which speed jet aircraft around the world; and by designing ships to be more efficient under regional and world weather and sea conditions.

All of these concepts are attainable within the present state of the science and their impact is important to naval operations as well as to commercial shipping.

The nearly limitless expanse of the seas and resources which they contain when compared to the crowded regions on land stir the dreams of scientists who are beginning to probe the last frontier of this earth. Many advocate the establishment of "sea grant" colleges where plant, animal, and human life on and in the sea could be encouraged.

Proposals to establish such a school program currently are

receiving active consideration by the United States Congress. Scientists also talk seriously of colonizing the oceans, both under the surface and on top of it. Aquanauts already have lived and worked for weeks at a time under the sea. Many believe that working colonies could be established deep in the ocean to speed the harvest of minerals and food from the floor of the sea. As the pressure for real estate continues to increase, oceanographers believe that floating barge communities of homes, businesses, and ocean-related industries could be established. Some have gone so far as to predict that these barges would be hinged to absorb action of the waves and the movement of these hinges would generate the electrical energy needed to serve the community. Fantastic? Not too much so. Even today a major watch manufacturer is exploring the idea of utilizing the principle of the self-winding watch to generate electricity from the action of waves.

The day may come when these dreams are realized, but the immediate oceanographic problems for the United States relate to the survival of this nation in a world where military, economic, social, and political competition is increasing daily.

The ability to completely understand the oceans, to predict their behavior, to use their potential in peace and war are essential to American security and progress. The national interest in ocean space has been declared by Congress as reflecting the need "to develop, encourage, and maintain a coordinated, comprehensive, and long-range national program in oceanography for the benefit of mankind, for defense against attack from the oceans, for operation of our own surface and subsurface naval forces with maximum efficiency, for rehabilitation of our commercial fisheries, and for increased utilization of all other oceanic resources."

As the late President John F. Kennedy said: "Control of the seas means security. Control of the seas can mean peace. Control of the seas can mean victory. The United States must control the seas if it is to protect our security."

But in order to control it, we must understand it.

147

CHAPTER SEVENTEEN

⚓

Tomorrow's Navy Today

The United States Navy, which will challenge the still relatively unknown world of the oceans and which will have the responsibility of defending this nation against political and military challenges about which we can only guess today, is now on the drawing boards of naval designers.

Oceanographers and shipbuilders, sailors and admirals, economists and scientists, doctors and politicians—all are striving to develop the type of ships and weapons which the nation will need at the end of this century. American naval scientists will explore the oceans from the North Pole to the Antarctic. They will probe the outer atmosphere and live for long periods on the bottom of the sea. Physicists will seek new ways to make nuclear power more economical and efficient so that the day may well come when the Navy is completely atomic propelled. Until that day arrives, some modern warships will be conventionally powered by oil. Mathematicians will work to improve computers and increase missile accuracy but, at the same time, guns may be returned for the deadly job of beach bombardment. Aircraft designers will build high-flying, fantastically fast jets which still are capable of landing on the short decks of ships, and in view of the lessons of Vietnam they may well develop more slower, lower-flying propeller-driven aircraft as well.

The efforts of these research and design teams will produce the ships which sail the seas and prowl the depths of the oceans as we enter the twenty-first century. It is too early to predict what these ships will look like, but naval designers are taking great interest, for example, in hydrofoils and ships that can skim across land and water with equal facility at nearly the speed of aircraft. The potential of these may prove the solution to the problems of amphibious and antisubmarine warfare. Others are developing extremely deep-diving craft in an effort to push downward to the deepest parts of the ocean the impact of sea power. Still others ponder the marriage of submarine and aircraft for the development of a flying submarine.

Although the immediate future in shipbuilding follows more conventional lines, stressing the expansion of the nuclear surface and subsurface fleets of much the same design as has been used since mid-century, the future in naval design is virtually unlimited.

In the decade ahead, the United States Navy will feature ships and aircraft much like those which have been added to the fleet in recent years, a period of tremendous advances in naval science. Here is a review of them (see photographic section for examples of many of these ships):

1. The USS *Enterprise*—nuclear powered, huge, and one of the fastest ships afloat in the world today. An armada of more than one hundred versatile aircraft operate from this self-contained floating airfield.

2. The USS *Long Beach*—nuclear-powered cruiser mounting missiles which can reach out scores of miles to destroy attacking aircraft.

3. The USS *Bainbridge*—also powered by the atom. Her long-range weapons can be brought to bear against aircraft and submarines. She is the last word in our destroyer fleet.

4. The USS *Chicago*—a guided-missile cruiser as modern from the waterline up as naval science can make a ship. Converted from a World War II cruiser, the *Chicago* is still powered by conventional oil-fueled engines.

5. Newest of the destroyer-escorts, designed principally to locate and destroy enemy submarines, feature coordinated electronics and operational devices to reduce manpower required to operate the ship. Remote-control helicopters and long-range sonar give the ship the ability to strike at submarines from great distances.

6. The landing-ship tanks, newer, faster versions of the old "large

slow targets," have a unique capability to transport large vehicles and unload them directly over the beach. One ship which can be run aground deliberately and back away without damage is the LST.

7. Working from the other end is the roll-on/roll-off cargo ship also scheduled for construction. High speeds en route and short unloading and loading time increase quantity of goods hauled port to port.

8. The fast combat support ship is truly a floating shopping center, offering the fleet all the stores, fuel, aviation supplies, food, and other supplies needed to keep a fleet under way in constant operational readiness.

9. A surveying ship, first of its kind in the United States Navy, will conduct hydrographic, oceanographic, acoustic, and meteorological studies. Navy-manned survey ships have the capability of producing combat and navigational charts to meet fleet requirements and also to survey beaches and land areas.

10. Under the sea, the USS *Thomas Jefferson* is typical of the new nuclear-powered submarine fleet of ballistic missile submarines. The nuclear submarines are more at home under the sea than on top of it.

11. In the air, the newest look in the Navy will be the supersonic variable-sweep wing fighter F-111B, also known as the TFX. At speeds of two and a half times the speed of sound, wings are swept back against the fuselage.

12. *Hawkeye,* one of the Navy's newest additions to carrier operations, the radar eyes of the fleet, is a turbo-prop airplane that proves the Navy still has room for propeller-driven aircraft.

13. Combining subsurface and air operations is this possibility: a submersible seaplane. Studies by Convair Corporation for the Naval Bureau of Weapons indicate that the development of such a plane is feasible and practical. On an underwater mission, the vehicle would be powered by electric motors and batteries. The three flight engines, two mounted on struts above the wing and a third located aft of the wing on top of the hull, would be sealed for underwater missions.

14. Coming back to earth, or at least the oceanic three fourths of it, the Navy continues its quest for faster types of surface ships and

the hydrofoil appears to be the answer. The world's fastest hydrofoil is *Fresh*, built especially for the Navy by the Boeing Company. The twin-hulled experimental craft is jet-propelled to speeds up to 100 miles an hour. Much bigger in size is the Lockheed-built *Plainview*, 220 feet long, 40 feet wide and weighing 350 tons. This hydrofoil research ship has a crew of 20. A practical application of the hydrofoil is found in the Navy's first operational hydrofoil, a patrol craft with speeds of more than 50 miles an hour. *High Point* weighs 110 tons.

15. Another new concept is SKMR-1, a hydroskimmer which hovers one and a half feet above the surface—ground or water. Built specially for the Navy, this is the largest air-cushion vehicle ever built in the United States. It weighs nearly 25 tons and is 65 feet long, 27 feet wide.

These are the ships which will lead the way to tomorrow's Navy.

⚓

CHAPTER EIGHTEEN

On the Threshold of the
Golden Age of Sea Power

Since the beginning of time, the seas, which cover three quarters of the globe, have influenced the progress of man—a creature who has restricted his life largely to the proportionately small amount of dry land on this planet. As the population of the world continues to expand at an explosive rate, the oceans become ever-increasingly necessary to our very existence.

These oceans will continue to be the traditional meeting ground for nations and philosophies in conflict, and the mushroom shadow of atomic warfare will make them increasingly important. The oceans, moreover, will continue to be the highways over which the goods of the world must move. As advancing technology demands more and more specialization among nations for economic survival, these sea arterials of commerce will increase in importance in the twenty-first century. And, as individual national economies concentrate on the agricultural and industrial production most profitable under the conditions of weather, manpower, and natural resources unique to each country, international trade must increase.

An exploding population's food demands are already skyrocketing. At the same time, the millions of people who are added to the world family every year press constantly outward for more and more living space. As farmlands are engulfed by the asphalt and concrete of cities, man must turn to the seas for new sources of raw materials. Aquaculture will assume ever-greater roles in the feeding of the people and the industries of the world, and the seas eventually may prove to be a place for a crowded people to live.

The true capacity of the oceanic world to meet these needs in the twenty-first century is still unknown because we have just scratched the surface of the sea in our quest for knowledge of the treasures it holds.

One thing is certain, however. The need for any successful nation to control these oceans will increase by leaps and bounds as the world becomes more and more dependent upon the seas. The United States must be an oceanic power of unchallengeable strength if it is to remain a strong force in the world of the century ahead. The sea power which this nation, or any other, requires to maintain such a position—that is, to control and utilize the oceans for security, economic, political, and cultural advantage—must be total power, balanced and complete.

It must include our foreign trade, imports and exports, commodities and services, and the cargo-carrying vessels of the merchant marine.

It must include the shipyards in which these ships and their naval counterparts are constructed and repaired.

It must include the harbors, the dock facilities, the warehouses which serve the naval and merchant ships as home or trading ports.

It must include the businesses directly serving our overseas commerce, the industries manufacturing the exported goods, consuming the imported materials, the rail and highway transportation which moves these goods to and from the ports, and the people who work in these plants, offices, and businesses.

It must include the oceanographers and other scientists who are penetrating the oceans' depths to unlock the treasure chests of animal, vegetable, and mineral resources.

It must include the fishermen, the oil-well drillers, and all the others who are actively engaged today in the harvest of the ocean's multitude of resources.

And, all of this must be protected by naval forces needed to guarantee the freedom of the seas so that we may pursue all these endeavors in the quest of knowledge, wealth, and future resources.

153

As the United States approaches the three-quarter mark of the twentieth century, its naval strength in maintaining the freedom of the seas will determine its national ability to survive and take advantage of all that the seas have to offer in the years ahead when political, economic, social, and military competition cannot help but increase at an extremely rapid rate.

The United States Navy's strategic missions in meeting the four-ocean challenge of the immediate future are: (1) Protect America's strength as a nation; (2) protect the United States from attack; (3) protect the movement of United States goods and peoples across the oceans of the world for normal economic and political intercourse.

The Navy–Marine Corps team can meet its commitments to defend this nation against all eventualities throughout the spectrum of graduated deterrence—ranging from friendly visits and showing the flag, through preventing or halting local conflagrations, to winning limited or general war. The Navy has available the tools with which it can meet each of these challenges.

The Polaris fleet ballistic missile system offers the United States an unusual opportunity to place its strategic deterrent forces at sea away from centers of population. Unseen nuclear missiles moving from place to place without causing so much as a ripple on the surface of the earth should cause any unfriendly member of the growing nuclear club to have serious second thoughts before succumbing to the temptation of a sneak attack upon this nation in a desperate effort to eliminate our nuclear retaliatory strength.

Aircraft carrier task forces, patrolling on the alert within striking distance of any trouble and yet always remaining in international waters, are ideal for extending the influence of sea power in cold-war or limited-war situations. The carrier task force mounts a great variety of surface and airborne weapons which make it the most discriminating force in the world today. Capable of dominating thousands of miles of the world at any single instant, the carrier attack force is also able to concentrate all of its mighty strength upon a single point. It offers the most varied choice of responses available in any single military force. The aircraft carrier is ideal

154

for blockades, for projecting striking power against sea or land targets, for support of antisubmarine or amphibious missions.

The nation must have the ability to place and maintain troops on hostile foreign shores. The Navy–Marine Corps team, equipped with high-speed landing craft and helicopters, is expert at assaulting enemy coastal footholds. The day is also here when substantial numbers of Army troops may be moved by the Air Force from United States mainland staging points to establish air bases anywhere in the world within a matter of hours. This capability will increase with the production of a new 750-passenger jet transport now under development. Ultimately, the nation may also see the day—already forecast by a former Marine commandant—when troops will be moved to trouble spots by rocket ships. Even with rocket ships, such massive airlifting of troops overseas would place a greater burden upon seagoing forces. For, overseas bases would be required to receive these mighty aircraft. If they have not been acquired, this would be the task of the Fleet Marine Force. If they must be built or repaired, this would become the responsibility of the Seabees. In any event, when such bases become available, the heavy equipment and supplies to be used by troops upon arrival would have to be transported across the sea by ships *in advance* of any movement of major Army units.

Major submarine attacks against American shipping can be expected in the event of general war. The Communist fleet of attack-and-missile submarines is numerically greater than anything the world has ever known. The Soviet undersea force is constantly undergoing modernization. The U.S. Navy, in response, is developing a three-dimensional force—over the sea, on the sea, and under the sea —to counter this threat; but the technological race between the submarine and the antisubmarine forces will be one of the hottest contests during the balance of the twentieth century.

The era ahead for the United States Navy is one of constantly increasing responsibilities. Naval forces traditionally have supported the foreign policy of all maritime nations, including this one. This is a natural and historic role for navies because they can move in

155

before tensions and incidents grow into conflicts and can do this without violating foreign territory or base rights.

The United States Navy, through continued growth and development, must maintain the freedom of the seas and the lifelines which connect this nation to its partners in the oceanic coalition of free-world nations. This will permit the merchant marine, through automation and other technological advances in cargo handling and ship operations, to restore health and vitality to this industry. It will mean that imports and exports can serve a healthy industrial community, providing the necessary defense and consumer goods for this nation and creating an expanding economy needed to meet a growing population.

The United States Navy must ensure that oceanographers have the freedom to unlock the mineral, vegetable, and animal treasures of the ocean depths and that the science of aquaculture is permitted to provide the food to feed hungry peoples. Scientists using deep-diving submarines and electronic devices must be protected as they explore and map the bottom of the sea.

The United States Navy has the ability to go forward to meet these obligations as the East-West contest continues for the hearts and minds of mankind.

Sea power is a matter of concern to everyone. Nations of the free world are too dependent upon each other to ignore the importance of the seas which surround us. Ours is a truly maritime society. Historically, this nation advanced the furtherest when its people understood and made the most of this basic fact, but today the very survival of our families and ourselves depends upon total sea power.

The United States is on the threshold of the greatest age of sea power and utilization of our oceanic resources that the world has ever known. This nation and its people must be victorious in the political, economic, social, and military competition for the seas which will face this nation in the decades ahead.

In order to compete, this nation must move forward on the seas. To stand still is to succumb. For no second-place honors are ever given in such races.

That is sea power and its meaning.

Index